Reflections on Perseverance

Growing Righteousness In Trials

Jean B. Burden

For further information, please contact Jean B. Burden

lilymom7@gmail.com

Reflections on Perseverance: Growing Righteousness In Trials

Copyright © 2020 by Jean B. Burden

Cover Design: Stephen Lursen Art

Cover Photography: Jean B. Burden

Published by: TEL Publishing, Charlotte, North Carolina

ISBN: 978-1-970094-04-6 – Softcover Edition

All rights reserved. No part of this publication may be reproduced or transmitted in any form or by any means, electronic, mechanical, photocopying, recording or otherwise without the express written permission of the copyright owner.

Scripture taken from Scripture quotations marked MSG are taken from THE MESSAGE, copyright © 1993, 2002, 2018 by Eugene H. Peterson. Used by permission of NavPress. All rights reserved. Represented by Tyndale House Publishers, a Division of Tyndale House Ministries.

Scripture quotations marked (NLT) are taken from the Holy Bible, New Living Translation, copyright ©1996, 2004, 2015 by Tyndale House Foundation. Used by permission of Tyndale House Publishers, a Division of Tyndale House Ministries, Carol Stream, Illinois 60188. All rights reserved.

Scripture quotations marked HCSB are been taken from the Holman Christian Standard Bible®, Copyright © 1999, 2000, 2002, 2003 by Holman Bible Publishers. Used by permission. Holman Christian Standard Bible®, Holman CSB®, and HCSB® are federally registered trademarks of Holman Bible Publishers.

Published in Charlotte, North Carolina by TEL Publishing. www.telpublishing.com

Library of Congress Cataloging-Publication Data

Burden, Jean B., 1958 –

reflections on perseverance: growing righteousness in trials

Library of Congress Control Number: 2020921085

Dedication

This book is dedicated to the granddaughters I kept and taught and loved throughout the pandemic of 2020. They helped me practice more trust, greater patience, and some technology tools I never knew I needed to use! When I asked them to name things for which they are grateful, every one of them said, "We are grateful for being together and being close to each other." I am thankful and blessed beyond measure. Our time together has made me a better person and a much better Grandma.

This book is for you. Thank you for your precious personalities that give me so much joy. October, 2020

"Consider it pure joy, my brothers and sisters, whenever you face trials of many kinds, because you know that the testing of your faith produces perseverance. Let perseverance finish its work so that you may be mature and complete, not lacking anything." (James 1:2-4, CSB)

Dear Readers,

What a year 2020 has been! If you're anything like me, your life has been changed, modified, and masked in ways you never imagined. We have isolated and avoided and created new ways of doing life, and through it all, the word perseverance has been on my mind.

When the pandemic of 2020 began for us in March, I was supervising students at Coastal Carolina University and teaching a class at Horry-Georgetown Technical College. Overnight --- or at least it felt like it happened overnight --- face-to-face classes were ended, and interns had to finish their work from home. I called one of my daughters and said, "If school has to close for a few weeks, I'll take care of the children. Don't worry about anything." Little did any of us know that my idea of a "few weeks" would turn to months. When I began to realize the foundational activities of life had been jerked out from under us and I would be teaching grandchildren from home through the end of the school year, I found myself suddenly overwhelmed. Ten-hour days with four little girls in four different grades with completely different assignments, and to top it off? We can't do what? We can't leave home or go out to eat or go to the gym?

Overwhelmed. For a moment . . .

Quickly, I found my way to God and said to Him, "If this is the plan you have for me at this time of my life, then let me do it well." In other words, help me, God, to make the most of my time with these little girls and with my husband and immediate family. Let me use my days well and honor you in all that I do. This was a big change of heart, but only possible because I submitted my drowning, fickle feelings to my Father.

As I worked on this new book during the pandemic, I realized on many days that friends and strangers have had to persevere through much more than I during this time. I have a son who had no work due to COVID, and I watched small businesses struggle to survive. I read Facebook posts of families who suffered losses from COVID, and most of them barely got a chance to say good-bye. Funerals could not be held and hospitals visits were a thing of the past. People everywhere have been learning to find a way to persevere through unprecedented challenges, and this became the focus of my heart as I wrote.

So, here we are. It's Fall 2020, and yes, I am still teaching little girls at home, though not all four every day. I have settled into a new pattern of living on Boggy Road, and God has blessed me in ways I never imagined to be possible. We have enjoyed many family meals, and my husband Dan and I have worked on projects both individually and collectively. We have turned a trial into a time of family and work and play and lots of Netflix! I've also used my time to write and study and take better care of my health, creating new healthy eating habits and walking with my dear friend, Becky. God has used this time to teach me to have some grit in my life: persistence about the things for which I am passionate, with the first and most important thing being my relationship with God, Jesus, and the Holy Spirit. I am amazed every day that God has the patience and love to continue to help me grow through the trials in my life and the days overflowing with blessings; I am grateful. This book is a reflection on the urgency of persevering with God through everything life throws our way. It is a book of GRIT: Growing Righteousness In Trials.

My prayer is that every single page will give you a thought, a challenge, and a friend who understands that when life presents its worst, we can stand strong against it all as long as we stay intimately close to God in every moment. I also pray that you will know you have a prayer warrior in me. You can reach me through my email (lilymom7@gmail.com) or on Facebook (Jean B. Burden); we must stand together as brothers and sisters in the body of Christ. This world may seem tough, but we are warriors on the winning side!

With love, perseverance, and GRIT,

JeanB

More books by

Jean B. Burden

Reflections From the Parlor:

A Pilgrim's Spiritual Journey

Reflections From the Pond:

Constant Faith from a New View

Reflections From the Porch:

Life Lessons from Boggy Road

All of Jean's works can be purchased online from Jean at www.brokenandground.com, as well as Amazon, Barnes & Noble, and most other online bookstores. They can also be found at Papa's General Store in Conway, South Carolina.

Table of Contents

1	Products and Promises	9
2	Tracks of Your Life	13
3	Lessons from Nature	17
4	Lessons from Cora and Fuzzy	20
5	Foolish for a Cause	24
6	Blending Pieces and Parts	27
7	A No-Stress Journey	30
8	Lessons from Fuzzy's Persistence	34
9	Perseverance Pays	37
10	Stop the Drift	41
11	Wasted Worry	46
12	Open Letter of Encouragement	50
13	Falling Into the Arms of Comfort	53
14	Being Contrary to Our Flesh	56
15	A New Pattern of Days	59
16	I Want to Do It My Way!	62
17	Garden Wisdom	66
18	Who Do You Call?	69
19	Lessons Learned from My Momma	72
20	A Fuzzy Prayer	77
21	Beauty in Brokenness	80
22	Patterns of Prayer	84

23	Losing Brownie	87
24	Dreaming of Flying	92
25	Satan Is a Liar	95
26	Lessons from Cinderelly	99
27	Flawed Characters	103
28	Stamina and Grit	108
29	An Open Letter of Prayer	114
30	Right Spot – Right Time	118
31	Gifts that Match the Receiver	122
32	Destiny Is All	125
33	Progress, Not Perfection	129
34	One Degree Can Make the Difference	134
35	Not In Our Nature	137
36	Dressing Like Mom	141
37	A 12th-Hour Victory	144
38	From Fear to Freedom	148
39	Submitting to a New Task	152
40	Perseverance and GRIT: Growing Righteousness In Trials	155
	Works Cited	160

Products and Promises

In the day in which we live, when infomercials are cluttering our televisions and social media space, products, programs, and services are a constant push. They promise success, rewards, and great service, and some of them deliver what they promise. Don't you love it when you buy something and it actually works, sometimes even better than you expect? I know that I do! In the past year I bought a new mop and a new vacuum. These were purchased after three years of trying to keep hardwood floors clean and three long years of frustration and daily hopelessness. Then I found these two items on QVC, took a chance on both, and my cleaning life has changed dramatically. Not only do they perform as promised, but they are easy on my tired back, and that's a huge plus! More recently, I decided to try Weight Watchers once again. I have used it twice before, and I did lose some pounds, but not enough. I got stuck and couldn't seem to make further progress. However, I have listened to the new commercials and talked to friends and family who praised the revised program. I gave in, decided to try again, and it works! I am truly amazed, and once again, I am thrilled to be able to say that the promises of a company are valid.

So, if we can get excited about a company that keeps its promises, how much more should we be over-the-moon about our God, our Father, whose promises never fail? We should be shouting His praises from the mountaintops!

What are some of His promises? Well, here are a few . . .

In Psalm 37:4, we read this: "Take delight in the Lord, and He will give you the desires of your heart." This promise comes to mind often during my prayer time; as I pray, I remind God (as if He needs reminding) that I delight in Him ---- *everything* about Him. I delight in His creation, His love, His power, His omniscience . . . I delight in **Him.** And so? I trust His promise that when I delight in Him, He will give me the desires of my heart. Now, let me be clear: my desires are not worldly like cars and houses and wealth. My desires are *His* desires . . . that my children are walking close to Him and serving Him, that my grandchildren know Him, that my ministry will flourish so I can speak of His greatness. It doesn't matter how things look at the moment of prayer; time is God's concern, not mine, and He will keep His promise because that is who is He is: a promise-keeper. He is *your* promise-keeper, yet, there's more.

I love warrior stories . . . Braveheart and Rocky and my latest favorite, Uhtred from *The Last Kingdom*. So, of course, I love the warrior image of God that is found in the pages of Scripture. Joshua 1: 9 tells us that we don't have to be afraid or discouraged because "the Lord, your God, is with you wherever you go." And there's another one in Zephaniah 3:17: "The Lord your God is among you, a warrior who saves. He will rejoice over you with gladness. He will be quiet in His love. He will delight in you with singing." I keep this one hanging in my bedroom because I need to know that *THE* mighty warrior is with me every day, rejoicing over me, His daughter. I need to know this on the good days, but especially on the difficult and painful days when life and Satan are hurling challenges and insults my way. I need to know this when I am fighting back from Satan's attacks on my heart and mind. He attacks with worry and doubt, but my mighty warrior God reminds me that He rejoices over me with singing. Don't you love the image that God is in heaven singing over you? I cannot imagine anything better! He does it for me, and He does it for you, too --- every single day.

PAUSE: I'm just getting honest here. As I am writing, I am struggling with something this morning, an unexpected fracture in my heart. I went to my journal to write about it, and song after song has played on Alexa, about God's strength and how I fight my battles with Him, but then I began to write this piece, and this song came on (from Elevation Worship):

"Your promise still stands; great is Your faithfulness, Your faithfulness.

I'm still in Your hands; this is my confidence --- You've never failed me yet.

I've seen You move --- You move the mountains, and I believe I'll see You do it again.

You made a way when there was no way, and I believe I'll see You do it again."

Wow, if you don't believe God speaks . . . if you don't believe that He is near . . . that He loves you as only a Father can love . . . well, you are missing the best thing in life. He has heard my hurt this morning, and He knows that I am trying faithfully to share His promises with you, my readers, and so He made it very personal in the middle of writing. Where is this promise in His Word? Well, it's in a book you probably don't read every day, *Lamentations*, and it says this in chapter 3, verses 22 and 23: "Because of the Lord's faithful love we do not perish, for His mercies never end. They are new every morning; great is Your faithfulness." We sing this song in church, but this morning the promise has been brought home clearly for you and for me: God is faithful, and He gives us new mercies every single morning. He has sent that message to us today through Alexa, of all things, but as I say all the time, God can use anything He chooses to speak to us, even technology. I needed to hear that promise today, and He, in His faithful love, provided.

When I sat down at the computer this morning, I thought I would write more, but the Holy Spirit has spoken into this moment, and nothing more needs to be said.

Great is His faithfulness. It's a promise to all of us. Might we be as faithful in our commitment to Him as we live our lives to reflect His glory as we were created to do.

Tracks of Your Life

On one of the early, almost-Fall days of 2019, when the weather issued an invitation to stretch my legs on our farm, I headed around our property with two of my granddaughters, Lily and Harper. We waded through some tall grass, hurrying toward the dirt road where "prickly things" wouldn't tickle our legs. On the dirt road, the girls noticed some fresh tracks, and we stopped to take pictures and think like scientists. We followed the tracks to their origin, the field next door, and we were able to tell where our deer visitors entered the road and the direction they took. We also saw dog tracks --- my Belle and Brownie --- and possibly a raccoon. Harper saw another track and yelled in excitement, but it turned out to be my shoe print. Ah, the joy of children! Anyway, as we continued our walk toward the cul-de-sac at the end of Boggy Road, it occurred to me that tracking the deer was an easy task. We could see where they began and the path they took, and it made me think . . .

Can people track where we began and where we are traveling as Christians in a world that needs some tracks to follow? Are we leaving clear tracks toward Christ and a life lived in holiness so others can follow us? And like deer, are we leaving tracks in the dark, maybe so others can be led toward the light of Christ? Let's ponder this for a few minutes.

Recently I heard a thought-provoking sermon by a pastor in Conway, Josh Finklea, at The Rock Church. He was preaching from Romans 12, and his premise was this: we must THINK differently so we can ACT differently. I completely agree. The scripture he referenced says it this way, " . . . be transformed by the renewing of your mind." (verse 2b) When our actions in the world show our thinking and our commitment to live more like Christ, then we leave tracks behind that honor God and emulate Jesus. So, what "tracks" can we leave behind? Well, there are quite a few but let's start with the obvious.

Track #1: Love - We are to love people, and our love must be sincere. Sincere love in the grocery store, in church, for the people we meet on the street, for our enemies, for people with different beliefs --- everyone! What a powerful track to leave behind in a hurting world where there is so much distrust!

Track #2: Hate – We are to hate what is evil and cling to what is good. We don't get to hate people, but we are to hate the things that are evil ---- I openly hate sex trafficking, racism, sexism, bullying . . . the list goes on and on. We must be clear that we hate evil; we *don't hate* the people involved in evil, but we hate the evil behaviors, loving the sinners.

Track #3: Hope and joy – We are to be joyful in hope (vs. 12). We live in a world that is not always filled with hope, so our attitudes must be ones of hope, grounded in our relationship with Jesus. We need others to see the tracks of a life filled with hope because we serve a God who never leaves us and who promises to fight our battles for us, if we will trust Him and wait patiently.

Track #4: Share with people in need. When we walk through our communities, are we known for sharing our money? Our time? Our resources? Do we share our listening ears for someone needing a friend? Do we share grace and forgiveness? Do we share what we have to make a difference in the life of another? These are tracks that fall right into the footsteps of Jesus. He took time for people, and so we must as well.

The list from Romans 12 goes on . . .

Tracks of blessing people who persecute us,

    rejoicing and mourning with others,

        living in harmony and peace with people everywhere,

            walking in humility,

                and a final big one . . . *never* repaying evil for evil, but always doing what is right in the eyes of God.

My mother was a loving, Christian wife, mom and servant. On the day of this writing, I am remembering her tracks, left long ago before she died exactly 34 years ago today. She left many tracks so I, her daughter, could learn from her steps and follow. She served her church, loved her family, lived in harmony at work, even when it was stressful, and never repaid evil with evil. She was kind everywhere she went, giving to children in need and sharing her time to help teachers in her vital job in payroll and insurance at the Colleton County Office of the Superintendent of Education. When she passed away after a brief and vicious bout with cancer, people spoke lovingly about the way she lived and loved; she showed her family, friends, and co-workers what it meant to leave tracks leading directly to Christ.

I pray that you and I are doing this every single day for those who need a path to follow, that will lead to the only light in the darkness – Christ alone.

Lessons from Nature

In the world of intelligence, Howard Gardner says there are multiple types of intelligence, and I completely agree with him. He says that we all have each type of intelligence, but some are stronger or more developed than others. My spatial intelligence is a -1, but my husband's makes up for it! My sweet Daddy and Mama clearly had a well-developed Naturalistic Intelligence, and so do I. I grew up watching them plant gardens and flowers, caring for them in ways that caused them to thrive. My Daddy could always give advice on how to solve a plant problem, and both he and my Mama taught me and modeled their intelligence and passion before my young eyes. I was hooked at an early age, and as I have grown, I have become more and more in awe of the things of nature. One recent morning, two things caught my attention: a mother cardinal and the condition of my plants.

Both desperately needed my attention.

I feed the birds that flit around our property, and in recent days, I have allowed myself to get too busy. I let the feeders become empty, and of course, the birds stopped visiting in front of my kitchen window. They're hungry *and* smart; they know when they're being ignored. In addition, the plants in my sunroom appeared droopy and pitiful. Again, my lack of attention to them. So, I set about making things right, filling the bird feeders and giving my plants a deep drink of water. Within a few minutes, a mother cardinal was back at the feeder, and my plants began to perk up in thanks. Both the birds and the plants made me think about our spiritual lives.

We often get busy and distracted, failing to give our spiritual lives the attention they require in order to thrive. But when we feed ourselves on the Word, the Bread of Life, and water ourselves with the Living Water, our relationships with God begin to recover immediately. We perk up, so to speak, sensing His closeness that was always there, but, we had failed to pay attention. We become hungry and dry because we lose the urgent disciplines of study and prayer, two pieces of our spiritual lives that keep us filled and hydrated.

So why do we allow this to happen? Just like with my birds and plants, why do we fail to feed ourselves with daily doses of God's Word and time in the presence of Jesus, the Living Water?

It's simple, really. Distraction. Busy lives. Losing our focus. Losing our sense of priority. Listening to Satan's tempting words: "It's okay. You don't really need this today. Go ahead and do the other things you enjoy. This is not important."

News flash: Satan lies and this is not *just* important. It is *the most* important priority in our lives. In order to stay truly filled and overflowing with contentment, peace and joy, we must feed and water ourselves faithfully.

Nothing more to be said because it is *not complicated.* In the words of the old Nike commercial, "Just Do It." Set a time --- make an appointment with your Bible --- write your prayers or pray silently or call out loudly to God --- whatever you need. But know this: when you do, He will show up and remind you of His great love for you. Just like my mother cardinal, who didn't complain about my treatment, neither will God. He simply wants us to show up to the table and be filled.

So how does this lesson connect to our sin and our service? Well, in ignoring God and placing other priorities above and before Him, we are committing a grievous sin. God told us on stone tablets: put no other gods before Me. Jesus told us to love God with our whole hearts, minds, souls and strength. *Very* clear. So, when we follow the command to love God alone, giving Him our hearts and minds, then we are able to move from sinner to servant. We can be strong in Him, finding the strength and direction for the service to which He has called us. Sinner to servant . . . a beautiful transformation.

Lessons from Cora and Fuzzy

I recently adopted two "rescue" cats. They were exactly what I needed on our farm: one-year old, (so my dogs will leave them alone!), neutered, and beautifully healthy. A friend of a friend had rescued them from her sick father, who was no longer able to care for them. She took them home, nursed them back to health, and soon realized she had way too many cats for her small living space.

Enter: Boggy Road Farm.

Their names are Fuzzy and Cora. I changed Cora's name from her original one that simply didn't seem to fit her personality. "Cor" in Latin means *heart*, and she quickly captured my animal-loving heart. But here's the interesting thing about these two cats. They are both very independent, and Fuzzy is even a little shy and skittish. It took weeks for them to warm up to me; I was smart enough to use food to draw them close. (It always works for me, so I figured it would work for them!). Now, Fuzzy scratches on the door every morning when she hears my feet on the floor. She and Cora have had a good night's sleep in their cat bed and are ready for breakfast. After they eat, they "take off" for the day, doing what farm cats do: exploring, chasing small creatures, sleeping in the sun . . . you get the picture. I can call them and hunt for them during the day; they are not to be found. They return at night, ready to eat again. I can hold them and they purr with joy, but they strain to get to their nightly meal.

And here's the spiritual truth that the Holy Spirit revealed from my time with these two sweet girls: we so often scratch on God's door, trying to get His attention when we are hungry . . . hungry for an answer, starving for strength in desperate times --- but after we're fed, we disappear to do what people do. Work, play, our to-do lists . . . the endless distractions of "farm life" in the world. We may not talk to Him all day until we need another quick fix.

This is *not* how God intends for our relationship with Him to work.

God created people to be in relationship with Him. Jesus came and walked among people to show Himself as Savior and be in relationship with them, knowing that His earthly walk and horrific death would save us all. And when He went to heaven, He left us another part of the Trinity to be with us, the Holy Spirit.

> Relationship. Relationship. Relationship.

Jesus is the Bread of Life, but He didn't come just to feed us a quick meal and watch us walk away. He came to be our Savior, our High Priest, our Friend, our Comforter, our Healer. God, the Father, is calling us to Him because He is a good, good Father who wants to spend time with us every day . . . *all day.* He wants to "walk the farm" with us as we journey through our lives. He wants to take every step with us in our quest to walk as His children, worthy of His calling. Ignoring Him until we need a quick "meal" must break His heart, as it would yours if your children treated you this way.

Putting the things of this world above Him is sin; putting Him first leads us to a hunger to be His servants. It's a simple fix.

I've made changes with Fuzzy and Cora that you and I can make in our relationship with God as well. Now, when Fuzzy scratches on the door, I open it and invite them inside to hang out with me before the meal. I hold them and talk to them gently, making sure they are confident in my love. I do that with God, too. I wake up and choose to seek His presence first --- the first fruits of my day --- long before considering or asking what He might *do* for me. I seek the Father, not His gifts. I seek Jesus, not His healing. I seek the Holy Spirit, knowing that when I study God's Word, having invited the Holy Spirit into my study time, I will more clearly hear what God has in store for me each day. I will discern things I might have missed before. Why? Because I have made my time with Him become the meal of the morning. And throughout each day, I try to call out to Him, just because I love Him, even when I don't need a thing. It's in this shift of mind and practice that we become less sinner and more servant. It's in our time alone with God and His Word that we will hear from Him with clarity about the work He is doing in which He wants our hands and hearts to be involved.

Selfish sinner to attentive servant. It's a relationship that changes everything.

Foolish for a Cause

I am in my 40th year of teaching, having spent 34 of those years in public school. I know a whole lot about looking foolish, and I can share plenty of examples. Example #1: I love grammar, and I was known for singing and clapping and stomping to help my students memorize rules about grammar so they could apply the rules well. Foolish looking, but for a purpose. Example #2: Every time a student learned something new, gave a courageous answer, broke through a barrier . . . all day every day, I cheered and greeted students with a loud celebration and high five. Foolish looking, but meaningful. Example #3: In my class we celebrated by singing the "Tooty-Ta" and doing ridiculous, loud things like roller coasters and clam claps . . . not a big thing in elementary, but I taught middle school. Very foolish, but a fun way to celebrate learning and children. Last example: For many years I took my students to Crystal River, Florida, to swim with the manatees. We were required to wear wet suits . . . enough said? A forty-something year old woman in a wet suit in public? Ridiculously foolish looking, but perfectly memory-making.

Following God and Christ can look pretty foolish, too, but when we choose foolishness for the purpose of walking closely with God, it is always worth every single, seemingly ridiculous moment. The Bible is filled with examples.

When God told Noah to build an ark to prepare for a flood, everyone thought Noah had lost his mind. After all, they had never seen rain, and so a flood was not even in their wildest imaginations. Noah was ridiculed for his foolishness, but when he and his family and the animals survived while others drowned, it became obvious that his apparent foolishness was actually faithful obedience to God.

Then there's a bunch of fishermen who left their jobs to follow a man they hardly knew. Foolish? Absolutely not. They dropped their nets, left their jobs and families, and spent three of the most amazing years with a fully human, fully-God Jesus, sent to save the world, involving them in His mission. In their wildest dreams they could not have imagined such a life-altering journey with Jesus; to some, they looked foolish. To us, they look like the faithful ones we want to emulate.

And in this list of foolishness, we can't forget Joseph, the husband of Mary. He was willing to be humiliated and look embarrassingly foolish to do as an angel directed. He could have divorced Mary to save face once he heard that she was pregnant, but he trusted the angel. He stayed with Mary. To many he looked foolish, but his decision to keep his commitment led him to being the earthly father of the Savior of the world. What foolishness and what privilege!

Of course, there are modern day examples. Francis Chan is a pastor, husband, and father who led his family to downsize in order to give more to others in need. In his book, *Crazy Love: Overwhelmed by a Relentless God*, he said this: "The concept of **downsizing** so that others might upgrade is biblical, beautiful...and nearly unheard of. We either close the gap or don't take the words of the Bible literally." Many people thought him foolish; he chose to take God and His Words seriously.

So, what are we willing to do, even in the face of foolishness? What are we willing to lose? To do? To give up? To build? To chase? What foolishness are we willing to endure because God says, "Trust Me"?

In Hebrews, we read about the cloud of witnesses, those who have run their spiritual race before us and are cheering us on our journey. They all looked foolish for their faith, and my hungry desire is to hear their cheers, be encouraged on my journey that may seem foolish, and finish strong. I want my children, grandchildren, and others in the world to say when I'm gone, "She did things that seemed foolish, but she always followed God, whose wisdom only looked foolish to those who didn't believe. She did believe, she followed Christ, and every seemingly foolish decision planted a seed for God's glory."

My epitaph . . . I pray it will be yours as well.

Blending Pieces and Parts

I have taught school now for forty years. (It sounds worse on paper than I feel!) When I began, there were no cell phones, no internet, no computers, and no SmartBoards. There was a chalkboard, lots of chalk and chalky fingers, and a single teacher in the room, trying his or her best to do it all as a lone soldier with limited resources. As the years progressed, I learned new information about teaching, new strategies, new brain research, and yes, the use of new technologies that changed my classroom experience. But here's what I always knew intuitively: just because new things come, it doesn't mean we throw out everything old. Yes, some things needed to go, and they went. As my principal used to say, "If the horse is dead, dismount." But some old ways mesh perfectly with new ways, and I was never one to complain as I learned new programs and new possibilities. My plan was to take the old, blend it with the new, and be the most successful teacher I could be. The same philosophy of blending the best parts came to play in my eating habits last week.

I've been trying a new program that requires lots of cooking and very strictly planned, healthy meals. It's been quite frustrating, especially because I don't love to cook, but also because the weight loss is not happening. However, I do see the value in having dropped sugar and other poor food choices from my diet. I decided, after much pondering, to take what I have learned and marry it to what has worked in the past: Weight Watchers. And today, the blend of the two seems to be working.

This is a great philosophy in many areas of life, but it is NOT a great philosophy when it comes to God's Word.

We live in a world in which, I'm afraid, people want to take bits and pieces of the Bible, only utilizing the portions they like and ignoring the rest. I also hear and see people choosing the parts with which their human minds agree and deciding the remainder must be too "old and outdated" to believe anymore or too out of touch, or the worst, simply a metaphor that doesn't really mean what it says.

News flash: our God --- Jehovah God --- Creator God – is the God Who *was*, Who *is*, and Who *is to come*. He is not outdated, and His Word is not a dead horse. It's a living, breathing, relevant document to guide and direct our lives. A field manual, so to speak. It is a book about relationships, with the single most important relationship being the one each of us has with Him, our heavenly Father, with Jesus our Savior, and with the Holy Spirit. It is to be believed cover to cover, from Genesis to Revelation, and when you read it and see it that way, you see the thread of God's redemption of mankind through every single word. We don't get to throw out the ones we don't like. His voice is in every Word.

But Jean, what about some of the things in the Old Testament? Do you seriously believe they happened? Yes, I do. But Jean, what about when God destroyed the earth? Do you still believe He loves us? Yes, I do. But Jean, what about a human Jesus who died and came back to life? Do you seriously believe that happened? Yes, I do, and in fact, it is the very reason I get up every morning with belief in His Word and hope in my heart.

Jesus died, Jesus rose, and Jesus walked the earth, having encounters with many people after His resurrection. It's a fact. You choose to dispute Him and what He did for you, but you are disputing history, and worse than that, you are abandoning faith.

We are told in Ephesians to put on the whole armor of God, not just pieces and parts . . . to "suit up" every day with the armor that provides the strength and truth we need to stand firm. And then? Pray over everything and stand. Stand still. Stand in God's strength. Stand firm in in His Word. Don't stand in the strength of government or candidates or worldly possessions or even self. Stand on the only immutable Word, the Word of God. Study it, ask the Holy Spirit to teach it to you, and then live it in your daily walk, a walk of strength made strong because you follow the God of the impossible. I can place my hope in this, hope that will never be deferred. I pray you will as well.

A No-Stress Journey

I travel quite a bit for work as a Coastal Carolina University Supervisor. I depend completely on GPS to guide me to schools all over Horry and Georgetown Counties. In one of my early visits of Spring 2020, I chose to go against my natural thought process, following GPS instead of taking a path I've taken hundreds of time. GPS placed me on Hwy. 22, leading to Hwy. 31 South; I was watching the time like a hawk because I hate to be late for a professional commitment. I questioned taking this path because it seemed out of the way, but since I know Highway 501 can be a traffic disaster, I took the new route. As I neared Hwy. 31, I had an "a-ha" moment: taking a longer, but more fast-moving route removes all stress from the trip. I was able to relax and enjoy the ride, knowing I would arrive on time. This experience reminded me of a spiritual principle: when we follow God's path as opposed to one chosen by our human, fallible minds, we can enjoy the journey so much more and eliminate worry and stress, knowing we're exactly where we need to be at exactly the right moment.

First lesson --- His path always produces a smoother trip through life. You and I can fight His plan and demand our own way and our own will, but our ideas and plans will never go as smoothly as the one God has ordained for us, His children. When we submit to His life GPS, we can relax into the drive, knowing we will be exactly where He wants us in His timing. The traffic flow will always be better, and we can find ourselves worry free. Yes, Satan will attempt to create worry, but it is easier to stay in peace when we know we have chosen His ordained path for our lives. Will there be bumps along the way? Yes, and this leads us to...

Lesson #2 --- Just when we think the sailing is smooth and perfect, something unexpected happens. On my drive, just after I had the "a-ha" moment, there was a major traffic clog when I moved from Hwy. 31 to Grissom Parkway. For a split second, I thought, "Of course, just when I thought things were easy, I run into a mess." But then I remembered that I was a few minutes ahead of schedule and one small clog was not going to ruin my morning. Our lives are like that, too. Even on the God-chosen journey of our lives, difficulties *will* happen along the way . . . family problems, illness, tough job situations, just to name a few. But those problems don't get to define our journey or steal our peace. When we know that we are on God's path for our lives, we can keep the peace that Jesus promised: peace that passes understanding.

This sounds very simplistic, and it is, but it does require decisions on our part. First, we must choose His path over our own. Second, we must trust His timing, knowing that He is never late and never early. Third, we must do as scripture tells us, casting any cares that arise on God because He cares for us. Fourth, when we run into problems, we must choose to persevere, continuing to run the race He has set before us. We do this by staying in close contact with God through his Word and through prayer. We also persevere when we commit scripture to heart, words that will support and encourage us when we need them most. Fifth, we must stay in close contact with other Christians. God places encouragers along our path, people who are listening to Him and are willing to share uplifting words exactly when we are in desperate need. These members of the Body of Christ can pray with us, listen to us, and be God's messengers with skin on. We should never presume to do life alone, hiding away from our Christian brothers and sisters who will walk the journey with us and hold our hands.

When I got very close to my school destination and thought I was home-free, I suddenly realized that I was working with an old address. I ended up at the wrong school. No worries, because I pulled over, asked for directions, and still made it to my appointment on time. God drove home the lesson of the urgency of seeking help when needed. I made a mental note for my next trip so I won't make the same mistake twice. God expects us to do that as well. We need to use the brains He has given us to learn from our mistakes and be more and more like the women and men He has called us to be.

One final note: I was grateful to have arrived on time and without major incident. A grateful heart will change the tone of our days and lives and draw us closer and closer to God, our Father.

I encourage you to step into the journey He has prepared for your life, allowing His GPS to direct your path. It will be a ride you won't forget!

Lessons from Fuzzy's Persistence

Recently, I received a new book about prayer: *Praying Women* by Sheila Walsh. I was reading early one morning, and I had just finished a section on persistence. Jesus told a parable about a persistent woman who continued to seek justice from a judge, even though the judge was unjust. The judge finally gave her what she wanted just to get rid of her, and Jesus uses this parable to tell us to be persistent in prayer with a Father who is not only just but loving.

Enter Fuzzy, my cat.

I'm reading about persistence, and I hear Fuzzy's "scritch-scratch, scritch-scratch" at the back door near my favorite prayer and study spot. She repeats her scratching every morning and every night until I give her what she wants: food. Sometimes when I open the door, she is there alone, and sometimes her sister, Cora, is there with her. Either way she scratches and waits every single day, twice a day, until I answer her request.

This is exactly how God wants us to be with our requests of Him, and Jesus made the same point in the parable I already mentioned. In fact, the parable begins like this, "One day Jesus told His disciples a story to show that they should always pray and never give up." (Luke 18:1, NLT)

Always . . . never give up. Strong and clear mandates. If Jesus was this clear about prayer, then we must trust that He is giving us the best lesson --- the best advice --- the best direction to take when we feel overwhelmed and broken and ready to quit. Always . . . never give up.

In 2018, I began praying about two situations that could have put me down, so to speak. Both involved my children, and both were the kind of devastating events that make you wonder if life will ever look the same as it did before. I prayed, and I waited. I prayed, and I waited. I prayed, and I waited some more. I'm not going to tell you that I prayed every single day. I should have, but admittedly, I let life distract me from the most important thing: time with God and persistent prayer. You see, these two situations lasted so long that some days, I simply let the rest of life get in the way of what I knew to do: spend time with God and pray. But then something interesting happened that truly renewed my persistent prayer life. A dear friend faced a similar circumstance with one of her children, and she came to me for love and support . . . mainly prayer support. She said something so important to me: "Jean, I prayed for your situation but not faithfully. Until it happened to me, I didn't truly understand the urgent need for persistent, bold prayers. I do now, and I am praying for our children like never before."

Isn't God amazing? He used my situation to place me in the position to help my friend because I understand her suffering, but He used her transformed prayer life to refocus mine for my own children. Today, my son has received, in the words of scripture, "more than we could imagine or ask," and my daughter's life is in a beautiful place. But here's the lesson: it took nearly two years of prayer, and even in my own failures during those months, God knew my heart. And He knows yours, too.

God is not a God of legalism. He is a God of relationship. On the days I failed to pray because I am human and flawed, God knew anyway. He knew the exact answer for which I hungered, the one I had lifted to Him in desperation and expectation so many times. And then, He did what He does best: He orchestrated the impossible for my son and yes, for his Momma in His perfect timing. I prayed the word "freedom" many days, and God gave us freedom in ways that are beyond my best hopes on my best days. What a good, good Father.

He is waiting to hear your persistent, "scritch-scratch" prayers today. The Bible tells us to knock, seek, and ask. It doesn't say to do it once; it places these commands in the present tense, telling us to do it daily. Like Fuzzy, "scratch" on the door of God, seek time with Him, and then, ask Him for the things that burden your heart and that will bring Him glory.

He is listening at the door . . . just scratch.

Perseverance Pays

I am an optimist to the tenth power, but sometimes, life is just stinking difficult, optimism or not. In the last few weeks, events have occurred (some of which I cannot share) that have thrown fiery darts of discouragement in my direction. I was holding up pretty well until last Friday --- then the emotional bottom fell out and my tears exploded in burning hot disappointment and sadness. On top of other challenging and gut-wrenching situations in my arena of life, I received a call that my brother-in-law had a stroke in the early hours of the morning, and things didn't look good. It was too much, and the tears began to flow.

I called my husband and probably scared him to death with my choking sobs, but I simply needed to share this heartbreaking news. You see, my sisters and I and our husbands are now the oldest of the family. Our parents and grandparents are all in heaven, and what we have, other than our own children and grandchildren, is each other. My husband was diagnosed with cancer about a month prior to this writing, and now my sister's husband is in ICU due to a "neurological event," as the doctors called it. I call it bad news. It turned out not to be a stroke, but it is still critically serious. On that morning, my heart felt as if it would burst, not just because these two men I love are facing serious issues, but because, on top of other problems and situations swirling around me, it finally felt like too much. Way too much.

I love being in my sixties. I DON'T like being at the age when I begin to envision my life without the people I love most. Don't. Don't. Don't.

Okay, I get it. I know the end comes for everyone, and we can never predict the timing of the end of this earthly life. I still don't like this feeling; however, I do know what to do.

Last Sunday, I went to church as usual, and it was an emotional service for me. I was still feeling the effects of personal challenges, but in obedience and joy, I studied God's Word and worshiped anyway. I sang, and I talked with God, and I thanked Him for everything --- I praised Him and I trusted Him. You see, no bad news will ever make me stop trusting God. In the words of a favorite old hymn – I never want to outlive my love for God. Never.

Then Monday came, and the most amazing things happened. I walked into my precious daylily garden, and my first blossoms were open. Not a big deal to some, but a *very* big deal to me. It was as if God was saying, "Girl, in the midst of your pain, there is always beauty from ashes." This first opening was made even more significant this year because the garden suffered so much damage and loss from Hurricane Florence. Then, another thing happened. I had a conversation with someone dear to me that, for lack of a better description, made my heart sing. I have prayed for this dear friend and watched her grow, and that conversation was like proof positive that she is headed exactly where God needs her to go. Again, it was as if God spoke: "Girl, do you see that I hear your prayers? Look at this young woman and be thankful." Well, I am!

Another thing came to light that is also an answer to prayer, but I think you get the point: when we persevere in faith in the worst moments of life and choose to love God and praise Him no matter what, He sees us! He knows we are hanging on by an emotional thread, and just about the time the thread appears ready to break, He sends the exact encouragement we need. A flower, a conversation, an answered prayer . . . whatever it is, it is a wink from God that reminds us that we are never alone, and we are loved beyond measure. Later that day I went to work with a song in my heart and a lightness in my step. No, my brother-in-law is not better, and my husband still has cancer, but God, my good, good Father, went out of His way to remind me that I am loved and that I never have to face life alone. Do you want to hear another cool thing…He did it in ways that matter to *me* personally; He knows us individually. The God who created the entire universe and keeps the planets in their orbits knows me and knows you by name. He knows what will lift our spirits, and then, scripture tells us, He send us His good gifts . . . just like a good Father.

There is a story in the Old Testament about Hagar and her

son, Ishmael. They have been sent into the desert, banished, because . . . well, it's a long story. Anyway, she and her son are in the devastating heat with no water and no hope. She actually moves away from her son, knowing that he could die soon. But then God shows up when her hope is about to break.

"In the midst of her despair Hagar suddenly heard a voice calling: "Do not be afraid; God has heard the boy crying. Lift him up and take him by the hand, for I will make him into a great nation." Then God opened Hagar's eyes and she saw the thing she dreamed of—a well full of water. In the midst of her difficulties, Hagar learned that El Roi (EL raw-EE) was watching over her and that He had a plan to bless her and her son." (Ann Spangler, Faith Gateway)

I love this story because it always reminds me that no matter what circumstance I face, God is El Roi --- the God who sees me. And in Hagar's story, God kept His promise to make Ishmael into a great nation...from hopelessness to abundant life. He does that for all of us every day. So today, no matter what you are facing, be obedient; praise God and love Him completely. Don't stop expecting Him to do great things or keep His promises because just about the time you give up, living water will show up and save your heart. Know for sure ... He sees you. He loves you. And, He will never leave you.

Stop the Drift

My pastor, Dr. Jeff Gaskin, recently delivered a sermon called, "Return to Your First Love." It was a powerful message to the church as a whole, calling us to repent and remember the power of life with Christ. Somewhere in the sermon, he said, "Stop the drift." It stuck with me.

"Stop the drift." Simple, but powerful.

I live in a town built on a river, and I have experienced being on a boat as it drifts downstream. I have led a snorkeling drift with my students in Florida; we drifted slowly and watched the fish swimming and playing underneath our floating bodies. I know what it means to drift, and the truth is this: I also know what it means to drift away from a relationship with Christ.

As a young girl, I gave my life to Jesus, making that long walk to the altar to tell my pastor, Rock Rogers, that I wanted to accept Jesus as my Savior. As a teenager and college student, I drifted away from church life for a season, but I quickly returned to the life and faith of my parents when I went home after graduation. Notice: the faith of my *parents*. I was faithful to church and service, but around the age of 40, Jesus grabbed my heart in a very different, very personal, and very powerful way. I had the big spiritual "a-ha" moment: faith is about relationship, not just religion, and in that moment, I began a quest to learn more and more about God and to give my heart, soul, mind, and service to Jesus . . . *for real*, this time. That was almost twenty-two years ago, and I continue to be drawn into relationship with God, Jesus, and the Holy Spirit every day. But there's always the danger of drift.

This may or may not be your story. Maybe you accepted Christ long ago or just recently. Maybe you had a burning in your heart that you thought would never be squelched, but then you began to drift. Drifting away from daily Bible study. Drifting away from quality time with God in prayer. Drifting away from church attendance because your cozy bed or time on the river pulled you just enough to keep you away. Drifting away from truth --- *the* Truth.

Drifting. Not running and not quitting. Just drifting. It seems innocuous, but it's dangerous.

You see, the problem with drifting is that it happens so slowly that we often fail to notice it. We slip away one decision and one moment at a time, and before we know it, we find ourselves feeling very distant from God. We didn't make some crazy declaration to abandon God or stop believing in Jesus; we just quietly let other things get in the way of the most important relationship of our lives. Quietly and deadly, and our drifting makes Satan deliriously happy.

The other thing about drifting is that we often don't notice the effects until we're in deep trouble. We stop going to Sunday School or Bible study because we're too tired or too busy or too "something." It becomes easier and easier to spend less time in God's Word, and when we are not in His Word, we are not learning about how to live *like* Him and *with* Him. Then, real life hits us, and we're not ready. Tragedy strikes or a serious diagnosis shocks us or our children go astray, and what do we do? We panic, we worry, we fear the worst --- all the things we don't *have* to do when we're living in close Communion with God, but we're not, remember? We've innocently drifted away from Him, and when we need Him most, He feels most distant. Lysa TerKeurst puts it this way in her book, ***Finding I Am***:

"And that's where the enemy wants us --- alone. Alone with our own tangled thoughts. Alone with his whispered lies that start to sound more and more like truths. Separated from the very people who could speak courage into our deep places flirting with discouragement and defeat. Separated from friends who could let us stand on their faith when our own gets a little shaky. The enemy knows if he can isolate us, he can intimidate us. Confuse us. Deceive us. And ultimately, make us believe that the safer paths in life are ones apart from God and our friends who serve God." (TerKeurst, 72).

Good news: drift is not permanent, and we serve a God who always has more grace than we have drift. In the story of the prodigal son, we hear of a father who not only welcomes his drifting son back home, but also runs to meet him with open arms. This is the image of our Father, God. His arms are wide open to welcome the drifters home. There is a beautiful story of Jesus giving Peter a chance to redeem himself after he had drifted away from faith due to fear. I love that image, too, because with Jesus, there is always forgiveness and redemption.

And one more thing... when we drift, we may *feel* far away, but feelings are fickle and untrustworthy. God has *not* left us. He is an omnipresent Father, and the Holy Spirit travels within us, even when we are doing our best to ignore Him. So, when we realize that we have drifted away and we are ready to call out to God, He is there. He is listening. His arms are wide open. Jesus, the light of the world, is ready and waiting to shine light into our hearts and lives once again. He is waiting without condemnation; He is waiting with a heart of love and compassion for His people.

Have you drifted away from God? Away from His Word? Away from fellow believers? Away from the single most important and invigorating relationship possible? Tell Him. Tell Him that you want to be close to Him again, asking Him to create a hunger for Him and His Word; open His Word and hear His voice. Ask His forgiveness for ignoring Him. Fall at His feet and simply say, "I need You."

Immediately, the drift can stop, and healing and restoration can begin.

Look at your life today . . . the way you spend your time, the way you isolate yourself from God and others, the way you convince yourself that God can wait until the end of your endless list of things to do. Ask God to help you see yourself and your situation honestly, and then let Him rescue you and draw you into His mighty arms. He has not drifted --- He is still on the throne. He is waiting . . . He is waiting.

Wasted Worry: Testimony from a Recovering Worrier

There was a study a few years ago about a topic that bothers tons of people: worry. Here's a quote from the study that sets the stage for our thinking:

"Lo and behold, it turns out that 85 percent of what subjects worried about never happened, and with the 15 percent that did happen, 79 percent of subjects discovered either they could handle the difficulty better than expected, or the difficulty taught them a lesson worth learning. This means that 97 percent of what you worry over is not much more than a fearful mind punishing you with exaggerations and misperceptions."

Wow . . . a fearful mind can punish us with exaggerations and misperceptions. I know this to be true. Just recently I found myself comparing my work and personal calendars with a little anxiety, looking ahead but trying to think in terms of one week at a time. You see, March looked almost scary with the amount of "stuff" on my calendar . . . all good things but still a whole lot of writing in those little blocks in my planner. I even reached out to the leader of an additional

Bible study I had felt led to add to my schedule, saying that I wasn't sure I could handle the amount of homework on top of my home Bible study and my Sunday School study. She encouraged me not to give up. I prayed about it, and then I chose to hang in there another week. I believe God led me to that study, and I'm sure Satan wanted me to walk away because staying means I can use what I'm learning to help others who need it most. In another situation, I was concerned about how much there was left to do in planning for a church event, and I was also feeling the tiredness and strain of work. And then in an instant everything changed. We are now at home, avoiding COVID-19, and everything on my calendar has been canceled or postponed.

What did that research show? Eighty-five percent of what we worry over never happens? Well, I guess this is part of the 85%, and God has reminded me of some urgent truth this morning.

Truth #1: Worry changes nothing, and we are not to worry about anything. In fact, He is very clear on this point:

"Don't fret or worry. Instead of worrying, pray. Let petitions and praises shape your worries into prayers, letting God know your concerns. Before you know it, a sense of God's wholeness, everything coming together for good, will come and settle you down. It's wonderful what happens when Christ displaces worry at the center of your life." (Philippians 4: 6-7, MSG)

Notice again what it says: don't worry . . . period. He didn't say not to worry about little things. He didn't say not to worry about big things. He said we are not to worry *at all*. But He did give us the perfect alternative, something that makes the difference: **prayer.** I want to create a mental picture of the choice you have.

Worrying = wringing your hands, feeling anxious, but getting no results.

Praying = giving your concerns to God, praising Him for His goodness, and walking forward in peace.

What a wonderful distinction! God offers us His peace in the midst of life's concerns, so we never have to worry. My calendar? No big deal. And let me be clear: had we not been asked to distance ourselves from others, God would have seen me through my calendar with no problem because I had placed my hands on the pages and handed the schedule to Him. As the scripture in Philippians says, I let Christ displace the worry at the center of my life. He filled me with peace, and as I am basking in His peace, I have been reminded of another urgent truth.

Truth #2: God is omniscient, and He knows things we cannot know or even imagine. He knew my schedule was about to change long before I did, but what He needed *me* to do was pray and stay in peace, trusting *Him* to work all things for good. In this time of "social distancing" and finding ourselves in a new not-so-normal, God *can and is* still working.

My husband and I just talked about how we can use this time wisely in our home. I am studying my Bible more than ever. I am spending lots of time with my grandchildren. In our worst moments, when we look to God, He can help us see ways that this time can *be* good, even when the situation that gave us this time is *not* good. God can give us blessings even in the middle of horrific circumstances.

So today, trust God completely. Do not worry and know that He is still on His throne, all-knowing, all-seeing, and all-loving His people. And this, my friends, is the testimony of a recovering worrier.

Open Letter of Encouragement

An Open Letter of Encouragement to New "I-Never-Planned-to-be-a-Teacher" Teachers . . . and Others

NOTE: This letter was written to encourage families, but every lesson here is a good one for each of us --- teacher or not!

Dear Friends,

In the last three weeks, many of us have found ourselves being e-learning teachers of our children, grandchildren, nieces and nephews, and maybe neighbors' children. We didn't ask for it. We didn't expect it. But we're in it, nevertheless, and there are some things I want you to know.

First, if you have moments of discouragement and frustration, give yourself grace. Teaching is hard in a perfect world, and this is far from perfect. Maybe, like me, you're trying to meet the needs of a large age-range of children. Maybe your internet is being sketchy, and they need it to load assignments. Maybe you really don't know how to teach them to do an array in math or a functional writing paragraph. Again, I say, give yourself grace, step away for a few minutes, phone a friend for help, and keep going.

Second, focus on the positive. I have started a gratitude journal, and it makes a huge difference. When our brains focus on gratitude, we get our minds off ourselves. Some examples of my gratitude list? I watched three of my grandchildren learn to ride bikes last week. I had time to share the Easter story with them. We are reading one of my favorite books together. I am watching them try new things and stretch themselves.

Am I tired at the end of each day? Oh, yes, I am exhausted. But when I focus on gratitude, it changes my mind and my heart.

Third, use this time to model and teach the children some life skills. My husband took our grands to a spillway between ponds; they had to figure out how to get across using some old boards and without getting their shoes wet. He got them to work on problem solving without adult help. Other life skills you can teach? Compassion, cooperation, listening, and independence. And one of my personal favorites, GRIT! When teaching them to ride bikes last Monday, the skill came easily to one of the three girls, but the other two had some difficulty at first. This gave me a chance to talk about having some grit when trying new things. It also gave me a chance to teach them that we are all unique beings, created by a wonderfully loving and creative God. We are not alike, and we do not learn at the same pace. We can't compare ourselves with others; we must love who God has created us to be and work hard to learn things that are important.

Fourth, get your children outside and let them learn from creation. Scripture tells us that creation testifies to God's power, and when I stood outside this morning, praying from my porch, I definitely felt closer to God. Take children on a walk, asking them to notice the things that are God-made, not man-made. Ask them to each choose a favorite beautiful thing, sharing why they love the items they chose. Just yesterday we saw a glimpse of our mallard hen with a string of babies behind her! We have waited on this for a very long time, and it was gratifying to share this moment with the children, allowing them to observe and learn from God's creative world.

And finally, pay attention to the children. When they are tired, take a break. When *you* are tired, take a break! Ask them to help you with chores in between schoolwork but make it fun. Give them lots of "recess" time, both structured and unstructured. I let mine put out Easter decorations today, and I celebrated every choice they made, perfectly placed or not. And most of all, love them and let your model show them how to love each other with patience and kindness.

I really believe that when this isolation is over, we and our children will be better for it. Breathe, relax, and do the best you can. It will be more than enough.

Love to you,

A Retired Teacher Turned Grandma-Homeschooler

JeanB

Falling Into the Arms of Comfort

I close my eyes, and I can remember the scene like it was yesterday. It was 1981, and I was grieving the loss of a much desired pregnancy. The baby died in the womb after a catastrophic car accident and a day of internal blood loss. Two of my good friends at church and my neighbor all announced their pregnancies not too long after my miscarriage, and my heart was broken. I was happy for them but fearful I would never be able to make that explosively-joyful announcement again. I remember going to my mother's house, opening the front door, and falling into her loving arms. I couldn't say a word, and I didn't need to speak; she knew my heartbreak, and she said, "You just want a baby, don't you?" I quietly nodded my head.

No words needed. She held me, let me sob tears of pain on her shoulder, and gave me comfort I desperately desired from someone who loved me completely and without conditions.

This is a beautiful picture of what God wants to do for each of us. He is waiting at the door for us to knock, enter, and fall into His comforting embrace. No words needed because He knows us completely. There is nothing hidden from our

Father. He wants to take care of us, and we need to run to the throne of grace and let Him do it.

In Psalm 62, we hear these words: (selected verses)

Rest in God alone, my soul, for my hope comes from Him.

He alone is my Rock and my Salvation, my stronghold; I will not be shaken.

Trust in Him at all times, you people; pour out your hearts before Him.

God is our refuge.

And then in Psalm 59, we hear these words: *But I will sing of Your strength; in the morning I will sing of Your love, my refuge in times of trouble.*

O my Strength, I sing praise to you; you, O God, are my fortress, my loving God. (Scriptures from HCSB)

God is indeed our Refuge, our Rock, and our Stronghold, and we can pour out our hearts to Him, our Father. He is both Warrior and gentle Father. He is our Rock and our soft place to land. Jesus is our High Priest and we can entrust our pain, our concerns, and our praises to Him. We simply need to allow ourselves to fall into the arms of the Divine and be comforted and strengthened. Just like my experience with my mom, we can simply go to Him . . . no words needed but to call His name. He knows exactly what burdens your heart, and He is the Great Physician, the Healer, the God who sees you and knows your heartbreak. Scripture tells us that Jesus came to bind our wounds . . . He can heal our hearts when nothing else can.

If you are struggling today with fear or anxiety, with exhaustion or depression, with sickness or loneliness ---- whatever you are battling, take it to the throne of grace. Jesus died that we might have abundant life, *not* a fearful existence. Go to Him, trust Him, and let Him give you peace that is beyond anything you can find in this world. Yes, if you are blessed to have a parent or friend-in-Christ who will hold you and pray for you, by all means, go to that person. But make very sure you go to the throne of God as well, with your friend and by yourself with your heavenly Father. And remember: if all you can do is cry before Him, it's okay; no words required.

He knows, He loves, and He desires to comfort and bless you. He is *El Roi,* the God who sees you. He is Jesus, the Savior who sits at the right hand of God to intercede for you. He is the Holy Spirit, who lives within you to guide and strengthen you. And if the Trinity were not enough, He also promises, when we ask, to send His angels to cover us. We can sit still, stop "trying" so hard, and let Him give us everything we need.

"Be still and know that I am God." (Psalm 46:10, HCSB). In the original language, "Be still," actually means, "Let go." How perfect. Let go and fall into the arms of Jesus.

Being Contrary to Our Flesh

Something incredibly strange happened recently. I've told you before about my wonderful rescue cat named Fuzzy. She is very shy, but during my time at home during the pandemic, she has become bolder and bolder each new day. She scratches at my door, hungry just to hang out with us in the early morning and in the evening after others have gone to bed. Just this week, she began letting the grandchildren pet her, and last night she did something dramatic.

Dan and I were watching television, and she scratched at the door. I let her in; she stayed a few moments and then wanted to go out again. I heard her crying outside, and it was not her normal cry. She sounded distressed, so off the couch I went, and I let her in again. Once again, she stayed briefly, and then cried at the door to go back to the porch. I said to her, "Fuzzy, make up your mind, girl!" Like she understood, right? Well, I heard that unusual cry again, and something in me clicked: she is distressed. I opened the door, and she dashed into the house with something in her mouth. My first darting thought was that she had caught a mouse, and I was prepared to tell my husband to handle it! But then I looked. It was not a mouse; it was a tiny baby bird. She dropped it gently to the floor and stepped away. She had not hurt it, and she did not try to take it from us. It was almost as if she was proud of bringing us this little creature who needed our help. Of course, the little one died in the night, but it left me thinking about the nature of cats and people.

Cats are natural bird chasers . . . bird killers . . . bird eaters. It is not in their nature to become distressed over an injured bird and take it to their masters for help. But that's just what she did, and now I'm thinking about us.

It's not in our nature to be kind and gracious . . . to love our natural enemy . . . to help when we would rather destroy. It's just not. We are sinful people who live by our fleshly ways unless we seek communion and fellowship and forgiveness from a loving Father and a suffering Savior.

Scripture tells us that when we accept Christ as Lord, we become new creatures in Christ. At that very moment we begin the process of changing: the process of sanctification or becoming more and more like Christ . . . more and more holy. He becomes our model for living, and we begin to learn what it means to live *in* the world but not *of* the world. Because of Christ's sacrificial love for us, we can learn to live sacrificially, which is not innately who we are. Because of Christ's forgiveness of all our sins, we can learn to forgive others, no matter what they might have done to us. *Definitely* not in our fleshly natures. Because of His model of humility and servanthood, we can be humble servants as well. Is this easy? No, it's hard because we are human and sinful and prone to live by our flesh. And yet, just like Fuzzy, we can go against our natural tendencies, and drop fragrant offerings at the feet of God Almighty . . . offerings of love and humility, of praise when we feel like giving up, of acceptance of His will above our own. We can do these things and more because when we accept Christ as Lord of our lives, He becomes the one driving our natures. The Holy Spirit takes up residence in us, guiding and speaking God's direction to us . . . directions about becoming worthy of the calling of being His children and co-heirs with Christ.

We can crucify the flesh, and instead of fighting our enemies and killing others with our hatred and jealousy, we can be like Fuzzy --- taking our unnatural, sacrificial gifts to the One who loves us best. We need this in our world today. We need love that is far beyond what we are capable of feeling on our own. We need kindness and generosity without measure. We need forgiveness that is only possible through God's strength and the forgiveness of an innocent Savior who died in our place to declare us, "Not guilty." He suffered the worst, so we can be our best.

Every day as you go out into the world, think about Fuzzy. Love your enemies. Be kind and help others whenever you can. And take your grateful heart to God, depositing it at the throne of grace.

A New Pattern of Days

We are in the middle of some unprecedented and trying times of physical isolation. In recent years, we have been home for hurricanes and even missed three weeks of school due to extreme flooding, but I have never seen anything like the days we're living right now. At first, I'll admit, I was a little concerned and stressed about being home and leading e-learning with some of my granddaughters, but God has given me a completely new perspective.

There is a spiritual experience called "The Walk to Emmaus," and it involves a 72-hour journey of being away from busy schedules, watches, cell phones, and calendars to give time completely to God. It is all about submitting to Him and letting go of the worldly expectations that often get in the way of our seeking Him completely and surrendering to Him and Him alone. It's an incredible experience, and this week I have been reminded of something that is said each weekend: the participants are asked to "submit to the pattern of the three days." This is an important direction since it is a pattern completely unlike our normal, busy, calendar-driven days. This phrase has replayed in my mind over and over since we began physical isolation from the world:

submit to the pattern of these new days.

So, let's consider this idea of submitting to a new pattern of days. Here are some things that I'm doing, and maybe you'll see similarities with your life.

- Spending more time with my family
- Spending quality time at the dinner table
- Slowing the pace of my mornings
- Giving more time to Bible study and prayer
- Taking daily walks
- Adding to my gratitude journal
- Cooking foods I normally don't make

The list could go on and on, but you get the point. We can complain about what's happening to us, and yes, this is a very difficult and trying time. But we can also see the glass as full, giving ourselves over to a new pattern of days. I must admit something: I'm afraid I will struggle to go back to the more frantic pace of life as it was before, and maybe God is trying to tell me something. Maybe you need to listen, too.

If your life is so busy that all you do is run from place to place and collapse each night from exhaustion, maybe you need to use this time to ask God what's truly urgent and what part of your schedule is His will and what part you have placed on yourself. Ask and He will show you.

One more thought: I was listening this morning to a powerful sermon by Tony Evans, and he spoke an urgent message. He referenced a story from 2 Chronicles, sharing how God allowed distress in the lives of His people. When the people called out to Him and repented during their distress, He answered and delivered them.

Sounds like something we need to do.

Evaluate your life, your time, your money, and your thoughts. Is God first? Is He the most important part of your life? Have you completely submitted to His will and His desires for you? I believe this isolation is a wake-up call for all of us to do some deep-dive soul searching with God. If we but ask, He will reveal Himself to us, showing us the places where we need to repent and remove idols that we have allowed to push their way into His proper place.

I hear it often said that, in our country, we have pushed God out of our lives, our communities, and our schools. Could this be our reminder to draw closer to Him than ever before? Could this be our time to pray like never before and surrender to His will completely? And then? Watch the hand of God at work in the lives of His people.

Don't let this time of isolation be a waste of days. Use it to deepen your relationship with your Father, your Savior, and the Holy Spirit. They are waiting for you and me --- waiting patiently --- and we must listen and respond.

I Want to Do It My Way!

Sometimes a life lesson is staring us in the face, and we simply cannot see it. Maybe it's because we don't *want* to see our own need to change, or maybe it's a problem with getting so caught up in a situation that we fail to "get out of our heads" in order to stand back and discover truth. This week has provided a perfect example of almost missing the point . . . notice, I said almost.

Recently I've been dealing with an incredibly frustrating situation in which my heart has been torn and through which Satan has fought to steal my peace. I won't share names to protect the privacy of my friend, but here's the gist of the story:

Friend comes to me for advice and help repeatedly.

- I give advice, financial support, and emotional investment;
- friend does as he pleases, ignoring all counsel;
- friend returns to me to "pay the bill," so to speak ---
- Bail him out ---
- Pick up the broken pieces ---
- Write the check.

Frustrating to the 10th power.

I've spoken with two pastor/friends, asking for advice, and they both have been blunt and helpful: move on --- shake the dust off your feet --- love him and pray for him, but don't, in the words of my husband, "be the solution to his problems." Hard for me, a person who likes to see problems and fix them. *Very* hard.

Yesterday I stood firm, refusing to give money, and what did it get me? A diatribe of ugliness screamed through the phone and a hang up from his end. Of course, he called again, and I was the strong but calmly quiet woman I strive to be: "You may NOT speak to me in this way, and if you do, I will hang up and I will not answer your phone calls anymore. You DO NOT get to do this to me ever again." It felt good. It felt right. But then this morning came.

As I was making my morning coffee, I was still bothered by whether or not I should have helped him last night, and I kept circling back to the fact that we have given so much over the course of the last fourteen years, and yet, this young man only seems to desire our "bail out" --- *never* our advice. He insists on doing things his way, and here's where the very obvious lesson rolled quietly into my spirit: don't we do this to God all the time?

God tells us in His Word *exactly* how to live. However, we have better ideas for ourselves, and we follow our own human, flawed paths. We fail, and then we run to God, crying out, begging Him to hear our prayers . . . fix our situation . . . lift us out of yet another pit of our own making. It's called EGO: edging God out, thinking we know better. EGO . . . it's all about us and not at all about Him. But, there's good news.

God does indeed hear our prayers, even when we have jumped into the pit of destruction and sin for the millionth time or slipped down an old slippery slope; He never loves us less because we have ignored His advice once again, but here's the other thing I know for sure: He does not desert us, but He doesn't always bail us out. Sometimes He allows consequences to be what they will be. He is with us in the midst of the mess, but He sometimes allows us to suffer the fall-out of our decisions. I feel sure He wants us to learn one of His most valuable lessons: "Listen to Me; I'm your Father for goodness sake, and I only give you sound advice. Stop trying to run your life on your own and let me be your Guide."

Oh, if we could only pass this test! God is perfect and good, but just like He saw the Israelites stray over and over and He allowed them to wander the wilderness for 40 years, He will let us wander as well. Now, He *will* stay with us. Do you remember that the Israelites had a cloud to guide them by day and a fire at night? You see, He was there, giving them His presence, and He also gave them Moses, but they didn't listen to Him either. They were stubborn and hardheaded, and so are we.

What is the thing you insist on doing your way? Is it decisions about your future? Is it your marriage? Is it how to treat others? Is it how to use the time you are given each day? What is it? How is EGO taking you to yet another pit of quicksand that is going to drown you if you don't stop making it about you and start making it all about Him?

How will you stop edging God out and instead place Him as your greatest priority in life? It can be done, you know. You can make a conscious choice to let Him be the Father you need . . . to let Jesus be the Healer and Friend you need . . . to let the Holy Spirit be the Guide you desperately need. Whatever you need, **He is it**. And even if you're in a mess today, stuck in the "miry clay," He really does want you to reach out to Him, and then…He wants you to surrender.

Oops. The whole submission thing. Yes, surrender, and when you do, you will be so relieved because trusting in God's plan and direction for you removes all pressure for you to decide, be in charge, and run the show. It's *His* show; let Him do His job. Let Him guide every moment of your day and your future, and when you do, peace will be yours. And what you will find is that you will begin to enjoy letting Him move all of your chess pieces because it allows you to trust Him, knowing that He will NEVER lead you astray. Let your Father's voice be the only one that matters.

Garden Wisdom

Yesterday, I worked in the daylily garden and throughout the day, I found some things that created a sense of awe and wonder. First, I found four plants that had been thrown from their pots during Hurricane Florence; they were growing in the middle of the daylily rows, thriving just in the dirt that was left around the roots.

Second, I found a beautiful plant, Benchmark, that was tremendous in spite of a vicious weedy grass that had grown in its spot and inserted its roots into the roots of the daylily. The plant had not multiplied, but it had survived.

Third, I found one tiny daylily growing in the most shocking spot. Last summer, I purchased a truck-load of soil for potting, and I accidentally bought the wrong soil. It was so dry that my pots felt like they held concrete; many plants actually died in their pots. But yesterday I found a lone daylily that had managed to grow in the dirt pile in spite of the poor soil.

Finally, I found plants that had survived in the pots with the bad dirt, and I replanted them properly with the right soil and fertilizer.

In all four cases, I did what a good caregiver does. I repotted the scattered plants in fresh soil and followed with fertilizer and water. I dug Benchmark out of the ground, separated it from the wild grass, and replanted. And of course, I took that lone survivor in the dirt pile, replanted it, and gave it a special place on my porch. I took every replanted flower and placed them in the daylily "hospital" so I can give them lots of extra care and attention --- which brings me to what's on my mind.

Sometimes we are "planted" in challenging spaces in life, and it's all we can do to survive. Sometimes evil creeps into our roots, trying to choke and destroy us. And sometimes we search for the light, barely making our way out of a dry season. In every one of these situations, God is watching and waiting, ready to put us in His hospital where we can recover, grow, and thrive abundantly. He is ready to keep us close to Him so we can get the extra attention we need. In each case it might look like we are losing, but the Cross reminds us that losing in God's world is only temporary. Easter morning is coming, and Jesus did come back from the worst possible outcome . . . it looked hopeless, but only for a few days. And, He did this for us, so we don't have to live hopeless or be destroyed by life's circumstances. With God, *nothing* is impossible.

But there's one caveat: some of my plants in the "wrong"

soil didn't make it. They didn't get my attention in time to be saved. Is this the case with you or anyone you know? Are you far from God or refusing to believe that Jesus is Lord? Have you ignored God's call to come to Him so He can care for you? We don't know how long we have on this earth, and one day it will be too late to accept His call --- to become a follower of Christ. But today is *not* too late. Consider what He did for all of us and respond to His love. It doesn't have to be complicated: just call out to God and tell Him you want to follow Christ as Lord, a perfect response to His complete sacrifice for us on the Cross.

Run to the Master who can heal you from your current circumstances and give you the right conditions to not only survive, but thrive!

Who Do You Call?

Years ago, a movie took America by storm; both children and adults could be heard saying, "Who you gonna call? Ghostbusters!" This is still an iconic catch phrase today, and it reminds me of something a friend of mine says. When we are together, praying in a small group, she will say, "If somebody wants to dial, I'll hang up," meaning she will start the prayer, allow time for others to pray, and then wait on the volunteer to close the prayer time with God.

Pretty cool thing. She knows, as I do, who to call in times of trouble, and it's *not* Ghostbusters!

When I'm sick, I know to call my doctor. When my internet goes down, I call Horry Telephone, hoping my son, Jake, will be the one to take my call! When I have a cooking question or need flower advice, I used to call my daddy, and when I need tax advice, I call my accountant.

So why is it we always know exactly who to call on the phone, but we so often forget to reach out to the throne in times of joy or difficulty? I think there are a few reasons.

First of all, we are filled with this sinful thing called EGO, and ego is all about us. In fact, as I wrote earlier, I've heard someone say that ego stands for *"edging God out"* of our lives. It is so easy to be full of ourselves and edge God right out of every situation. We do well at work, and we throw ourselves a party. We run into a problem, and we try to "fix it," desperately scrambling to manage the situation under our own steam when God's solutions are always so much better. Ego can get us into self-centered trouble when it edges God out of His rightful place as our sole priority and the center of all that we are. But I think there's even more.

I don't know about you, but my calendar is a real issue. I find myself bowing to the scheduled items of each day, and it's easy to say, "I'll pray when I get home, or I'll pray more tomorrow." It's especially hard when we need to leave home early; sometimes I pray in the car, and that's okay, but it's not the same as being still before a holy God or falling on my face in repentance and submission. We are letting events control how much time we spend with God, but He *always* makes time for us. Why can't we do the same?

We are living in the middle of the COVID-19 pandemic, and one of the things that has happened for many of us is a dramatic slow-down. We aren't going *anywhere*; we aren't planning events; we aren't doing anything that places us at risk. I am a professor, and I have switched from college courses to homeschooling elementary and preschool grandchildren. Talk about a change of pace! And through every bit of it, I have felt a very strong sense of gratitude for the time at home. Don't misunderstand what I'm saying: I love my job, and I adore my students. I know that what I do helps young people, and I am deeply grateful that in year forty of teaching, I am still going strong. However, I have also learned to love the slower days and the privilege of deciding my own schedule and my own pace of things, starting with prayer, study, and lots of coffee. My church started a 24-hour a day unbroken prayer vigil, and I begin my day with that every single morning. I don't have to feel rushed, and I surely don't need to dress for work! I simply get to sit with a holy and sovereign God, praise His name, repent of my sin, intercede for the many needs in our world, and yield to His will. I can *never* remember a time in my life when I've had this much freedom and time with God.

Who am I calling? God ... Father ... Provider ... Comforter ... Healer ... Sovereign, Almighty God!

"Who you gonna call?" My prayer is that we are praying in concert from our isolated homes to our same Father and Savior and listening to the same Holy Spirit. He must be the centerpiece of your calendar every day, and He is waiting to hear your voice. Just like the Ghostbusters rid the world of ghosts, He can rid your world and heart of fear, anxiety, depression and any other "ghost" that is trying to trouble you. And, in the words of a favorite song and a book by the same title, the battle belongs to the Lord!

Lessons Learned from My Momma

Just before social isolation became a new part of our lives in 2020, I had to let go of my dog, Brownie. Trying to help myself and my grandchildren deal with the loss, I read them a book called *The Tenth Good Thing About Barney*. It's a story of a cat who dies, and the child who misses him writes ten good things about him to share as they remember his life. Just this past week, Lily, one of my granddaughters, finished reading the book *Because of Winn Dixie*. In the book, the central character's mom left her; she talks with her father, the preacher, trying desperately to remember ten good things about her mom.

Remembering is important, and this morning during my time with God, I began to ponder how much I missed by living my grown-up years without a mother. The conversations I missed. The joys I missed. The comfort I missed. The privileges I missed of being her daughter as I grew up enough to truly appreciate her for the woman she was. And in the midst of my tears, it occurred to me that writing some good, faith-based things about her could be good for me and for you, my readers. She was a woman with a lot to offer.

And so, I write, following the style of two authors I love,

Judith Viorst and Kate DiCamillo. Thank you for being my inspiration.

Number 1: My Momma raised me in church. In this day and age, some of you will say that's a bad or unnecessary thing, but let me tell you why it's a foundational practice. "Church" is an imperfect place with imperfect people, but she made sure I grew up knowing the Bible. I hung out with youth group and had worlds of fun. I attended Girls in Action and learned about growing in love, giving my GA Coronation speech on the 2 Corinthians passage on love. I learned to love music, and I learned how to sing. By the age of eight, I was playing handbells, and I have been singing in some kind of choir since I was five. My church allowed me to begin using my piano skills by the time I was 11 or 12. I was baptized by a man named Rock, and as a young adult I was comforted by a pastor named Posey . . . comforted through the loss of my first child and the loss of my mother. None of these things would have EVER happened had my mother not given me a foundation of church, which has led to a foundation in Christ, the most important part of my life.

Lesson #1: *We need a foundation built by learning and growing with other Christians in a healthy church that teaches God's Word. We also need to allow our children to find places of service, even when they are very young.*

Number 2: My Momma was an amazing cook. Her kitchen was the tiniest little work space, but the dimensions of the room never diminished the size or perfection of her Southern meals. Her scalloped potatoes were the food of legends, at least in the minds and hearts of our family, and she made banana pudding that I can still taste in my memory. She always left the table early so she could make it fresh and hot . . . we *never* ate cold pudding! Add to these two dishes her Christmas sweets, her fried chicken, and her homemade, slighty-lumpy mashed potatoes, and you find a daughter who grew up loving Southern food ... *way* too much of it. I will always be grateful for the spread she shared willingly every day, and especially her Sunday family dinner. She created a safe space to eat, laugh, and just hang out when the meal was over. I loved being a child at her table.

Lesson #2: *Just like my mother used her gift of cooking to bless others, we must use our gifts generously to bless our families and others around us.*

Number 3: My Momma was one of the hardest workers I have ever known, and her integrity and work ethic taught me volumes about how to give my best to the students in my care. She worked in the office of the Superintendent of Education of Colleton County, and she spent her entire adult life taking care of the concerns of teachers. She did payroll and managed the teachers' insurance. Once I watched her help a dying teacher get her affairs in order so her children would be okay once she passed. After my Momma died, teachers throughout our district shared so many gracious things with me about her, but one that sticks with me to this day is this: "If you had a concern and you took it to Ms. Rosine, you never had to think about it or worry about it again. It would be handled, and it would be done right." There aren't a whole lot of people in the world who could put that on their tombstone: *trusted to do what she promised. Always.* I am in my 40th year of teaching, and I have modeled my teaching career after her work ethic.

Lesson #3: *Be a person on whom others can count to do what is promised. God expects us to work and live with integrity that comes from His perfect integrity in dealing with His people.*

Number 4: My Momma knew how to love…unconditionally, quietly, with words and without. She loved deeply, and I never once wondered if she loved me. Frustrated with me from time to time? Oh, you better believe it, but I somehow understood that her frustration never changed her love for me. She loved like Christ. I rode with her in the car while she delivered clothes and other items to children in need. I watched her serve in her church because she loved church, but mostly, she loved Christ. She loved. Period. When she watched the baptism of my nephew, Wes, she cried, saying, "This is the last one of these I will ever see. I will never see your children being baptized." She was dying, and she loved her grandchildren and wanted to see the memorable moments in their lives, both big and small. I hope she sees from heaven.

Lesson #4: *Jesus commands us to love: love God first with our hearts, minds, souls, and strength, and love others as* *ourselves --- love unconditionally, love our enemies, and love without judgment. Love and let it be the driving force of your life.*

And that, my friends, is the end of the lesson.

A Fuzzy Prayer

This morning I prayed for my cat, Fuzzy. In the middle of COVID-19 and people being out of work, it seems like a selfish and petty prayer. I prayed it anyway because somewhere in the wealth of things I know about God, I know this: what matters to me, His daughter, matters to Him. So, I prayed. There's a story that He needed to show me.

Fuzzy is my consistent cat; she claws at the backdoor every single day, somewhere between 5:00 and 5:30 AM, and she returns to ask for admission again in the evening after dinner. She likes the atmosphere of the house when things are quiet . . . no children yelling and running. She wants to eat, sleep in her spot of the day (it changes daily), and just hang out. Then she cries to go out, and we repeat the routine tomorrow. But a few days ago, she didn't show up to scratch on the door, and my heart sunk.

During this COVID-19 crisis, I have relished the slower routine of days, and Fuzzy's consistent "scritch-scratch" at my door has become a small piece of comfort. I love to hold her, listening for her loud purr and appreciating her companionship. When she didn't show up, I knew something was wrong. Yesterday she came back, but only in the evening, and again this morning, she didn't ask for her early morning entry. I'll admit that it disturbed me because she has become more than a companion; she has allowed me over the course of many months to gently create a trusting bond between us. I have said to her and her sister Cora over and over, "I am so grateful for you and your sweetness. I am blessed and happy that you came to live with us."

Then she disrupts the routine I have come to know and love. And so, this morning, I prayed for her safe return. Just a few minutes ago, I looked out the window of my office, and there she was. I flew to the door, scooped her into my arms, and welcomed her home! I also thanked God for answering my prayer . . . not selfish or petty . . . a prayer of my heart, and He used it to give me something to share.

During this time of isolation, some of you have been just like Fuzzy. You have scratched at the door of heaven regularly, seeking time with God. Some of you haven't. You've allowed the disrupted routine of being home more than normal, possibly with children needing an education, to take over your schedule. Somewhere you've lost the precious appointment time with God. But just like I felt with Fuzzy, I didn't care that she seemed to forget me for a few days; I was ecstatic to see her on the porch, and I welcomed her into the Boggy Road fold with complete love and acceptance.

God is waiting on you with open arms, too.

Years ago, I heard a pastor use the word "wooing" when

talking about God, and I have never forgotten it. (Thank you, Steve Lemons!) God, Jesus, and the Holy Spirit are always wooing us into relationship. Sometimes it happens through an answered prayer; when God answers the cries of my heart, I feel like He is speaking just to me, and I draw closer to Him. Sometimes it happens when I am captured by the majesty and beauty of nature. I can sit on my porch quietly, being intentional about noticing every detail of life around me and then know that God is present and an omnipotent Creator. Sometimes He woos us through a "wink." Just yesterday, I tuned into a pastor on YouTube, and the message he shared was exactly what someone in my family needed to hear. She was in the kitchen, cooking breakfast, and she was in the right place: exactly where the Holy Spirit needed her to be when He sent that message of complete love and acceptance. He wooed me even closer to Him because I saw His love for *her*.

Wooing . . . calling . . . waiting with open arms for our scratch at the door of heaven. He never tires of hearing our voices because we are His children . . . His heirs. And just like I love hearing Fuzzy's scratch at my door, God loves hearing your voice, calling His name because you want to enter His presence and spend time with your Father. Don't be like Fuzzy: don't let the days go by when you fail to show up for your personal and sacred time with God. Let Him woo you into His presence, and then be eternally grateful that He always welcomes you home . . . no matter how long you've been away.

Beauty in Brokenness

I walked on the beach this morning. I went very early, hoping to find some sharks' teeth but to no avail. However, I did find some beautiful shells --- some perfect without a single blemish or crack and others, broken fragments of what once was. The more I walked and looked, the more I thought about God, the Creator of the ocean and its inhabitants. As my eyes watched the waves coming in and going out and the expanse of the horizon, I thought of God's plan and His perfection.

I went to the beach looking for one single thing, but in looking for something that never materialized, I found something beautiful. Life with God is just like that. We, in our human minds, are looking for that perfect job, that ideal situation, or that next promotion, but God often has something way more valuable that He needs us to find instead. In my own life, I remember being Horry County Schools District Teacher of the Year. I prayed and prayed, believing that God was going to allow me to be SC State TOY or at least in the Top 5; it was not to be. I cried when the "no" arrived in the mail and left school that year not sure I would still have my passion when I returned in August. But true to a good Father with a perfect plan, God knew I didn't need to win that title. He needed me right where I was; I just couldn't see it at the time. The year prior to my win, our school was in the running for a major state award; we didn't win but were encouraged by judges to try again; little did I know that the next year would be our victory. We would be the little school that could . . . from struggling to one of the best in the state, and because I did not win State TOY, I was there to be an integral part of that hard work and the thrilling victory. God knew exactly where I needed to be, and He knows that about your life as well. Following Him requires trust and surrender, and sometimes we must suffer defeat and even cry for a bit; but then we get back on our feet and do our best as He puts His plans in place. Perfect plans. Plans that we couldn't see on the horizon. If you are feeling defeated or disappointed today, grieve the loss and surrender to a holy God with a plan that has been in place for your life since before you were born. Read Jeremiah 29:11 . . . God knows the plans He has for you . . . to prosper you and give you hope and a future.

And, there's more. As I searched for the sharks' teeth that never came, I started to see a pattern of shells . . . a pattern of perfection and a pattern of brokenness. Just like the Garden of Eden's perfection, God created each one of these shells, perfectly shaped and designed for the mollusk it would house. But then the waves and the sand took their toll on these perfect shells, and many of them shattered. Isn't that a pattern with us, too? We start our lives, perfectly designed for what God has in store for us, but then we mess things up. We run up against waves and sand called sin, disappointment, and loss, and in the process, we find ourselves broken. But here's the best news of all: the broken shells are still beautiful, showing swirls, ridges, and colors, and in some of the broken pieces, we actually get to see the inside of the shell. Brokenness in life can do that to us, too. It can break us until others see what's truly inside each one of us, and it can be transformative. God can take our broken pieces, forgive and heal us by His grace, and use our experiences with brokenness to place beauty on the beach of our lives so others can find healing, too. Perfection is nice, but it's overrated and unattainable. Brokenness gives God a chance to heal us from the inside out and use us to share beauty with others if we trust Him and surrender. A pattern, isn't it?

There's one more thing. When I headed out to the beach this morning, I took too many things with me. I thought I was fine . . . coffee cup in hand with the perfect lid to block the sand and my cell phone tucked into the waist band of my shorts. My glasses were on the top of my head, and I had my key ring around my wrist. It wasn't too long before the wind and the glasses went to war, and my sandals had to be removed. My phone kept slipping lower and lower, and I spilled my coffee on my shirt more than once. Finally, I found a dry spot and left everything behind except my glasses. It was then that I could focus on the task at hand, and during my shell search, God gave me a revelation: sometimes in life we try to take too many things and people and ridiculously filled calendars into the plans He has prepared. We find ourselves burdened and dropping the most important pieces He is giving us. So how do we know what to put down? Well, we pray and ask and listen. He is faithful to guide and show us the way to go, even sometimes telling us to leave things behind. That wonderful school where I won District Teacher of the Year? In 2012, He told me to leave... to trust my principal and follow her to a new job. I loved it there, and every year had been a blessing, but it was time to go, and so in obedience and complete trust, I went. A number of years ago, God told me to leave a church position that had blessed me beyond measure. I had to leave friends and a pastor behind, and I still miss them to this day, but I was holding on to too many things to be able to do the next things He had in store, and so it was time to let go.

Where are you today? Are you exactly where God needs you to be? Wonderful! Stay put until He says something different, but if you are searching and questioning, then listen and if He says it's time to go, then surrender and go. He just might have a place you can use the broken pieces of your life to bless others who need you to walk beside them and show them that with God, they can survive and thrive. God has allowed some tough situations in recent years, but through these hard times, He has grown and changed me, and quite honestly, I may have been broken, but as I said before, perfection is overrated. God can't really use my perfection; He did that with His Son. But He can surely use my imperfections to spread hope everywhere I go.

Blessed to be broken and beautiful!

Patterns of Prayer

I talk to people often who are confused about how to pray. Some people just don't know where to start or have crazy expectations of what God expects during prayer. I want to give you two acronyms that basically give you same the prayer pattern; you may find these helpful even if you are comfortable in prayer and have been praying for a long time.

#1: PRAY = Praise, Repent, Ask, and Yield

#2: ACTS = Adoration, Confession, Thanks, and Supplication

Notice that both begin with praising and adoring God. When I talk with Him, I praise Him before I ever ask for anything, and praising is very different from thanksgiving. When I praise, I talk to Him about who *He is* . . . Creator, Deliverer, Sustainer, Father . . . It's not about me --- only about Him. Then I offer specific thanksgiving for the blessings I have received from Him. I thank Him for everything, big and small.

Next, I repent, or confess. I love doing this next because I feel like it clears my heart as I approach a holy God. I don't want to sit in His presence soaked in sin, and so I confess it to Him early my prayer time. Yes, He already knows everything, but when I confess and repent, I am not only asking forgiveness, but I am making a turn in an opposite direction. As part of my confession, I always ask Him to show me anything I have failed to confess --- any darkness in my human heart that I've missed. And then?

I ask. (In the ACTS acronym, this is called supplication.) I ask boldly and joyfully and with expectation. I ask humbly and with a submitted heart and mind. I ask Him to help me be patient and wait on His answers, which are always better than mine. I ask for perseverance in my challenges, and I ask Him to keep me in peace while I wait. I ask for discernment as I study scriptures, and I ask for help with every task of my day. I also ask for healing and answers for other people; this type of prayer is called intercession, and I love interceding for others. Just this morning before I started writing, one of my students reached out to me by text. Before we ended our conversation, I asked if I could pray for anything for her, and she quickly responded, "Yes." And so, I included her requests for healing in my asking. Scripture promises that when we ask, God hears from heaven and answers our prayers.

And finally, following the PRAY acronym, I yield. What does that mean? Well, for me, it means to surrender to anything and everything God asks . . . if He asks me to wait, I must wait. If He asks me to let go of an offense or unforgiveness, I must yield to that, too. And if He asks me to be kind to my enemies . . . and He will . . . then I must. Yielding is all about surrendering and submitting to whatever God's plan and purpose is for our lives. I always ask Him to help me surrender in humility and grace, especially when I don't understand His plan and cannot see what He is doing behind the scenes or what situations He might be orchestrating for my good. Yielding . . . it's all about trusting the God who created us in His image and but also uniquely who He fearfully and wonderfully designed us to be.

And so we PRAY: praise, repent, ask and yield, and I trust completely that every prayer is heard for you and me by the Father who loves us and the Savior who sits at the right hand of God, whispering our names into His ears: "God, do you hear Jean? God, do you hear . . . ? They're calling you . . ."

Losing Brownie

If you've read my book, *Reflections from the Porch* (2019), you know a little about my boy, Brownie. He's the dog who showed up, found a safe place with us, and never left. After months of hanging on the fringes of our property, allowing us to feed him but not touch him, he finally wanted physical warmth, a desire that overcame his fear of people, and we found him huddled in our garage. He wanted physical warmth from the cold; what he received was love beyond measure --- an emotional warmth he needed more than anybody knew. He has gone from being a distant guest to being Brownie, "our boy."

A gift we never expected and one that was better than anything we could have asked to receive. Kind, loving, tender, and gentle. A gentle giant Labrador who needed us and we have surely learned to need him.

Brownie is dying. We found out unexpectedly when I took him to the vet for what I thought might be a problem with a snake bite or something he ate . . . something fixable. When the vet tech invited me into the examination room, I laughingly said, "Ok, tell me what got him." What happened next took my breath and unleashed my tears. Lymphoma, the vet said. Not fixable. And just like that, cancer is stealing from my life again. It took my mom, it attacked my husband last year, and now Brownie. God blessed me with a wonderful vet, Hugh Strickland, and his staff of loving techs. They let me cry, and one of the girls even talked to my husband by phone, explaining the situation. We could say good-bye that day, allowing the vet to help us transition him, or we could complete a course of prednisone, giving him what would appear to be remission, buying us time to prepare as a family to let him go. We opted for time.

In my conversation with the staff, I shared how Brownie inserted himself into our lives and even into my last book, and then the vet asked a question: "Will you write about this, too?"

"Yes, I guess I will," I responded. And here we are. In my most recent Bible study, the author, Lysa Terkeurst, said this: "All broken things are subject to restoration." Well, my heart is breaking; the collective heart of my family is breaking. It's more than just losing a good dog. Brownie was an unexpected gift who showed up to bless us in unimaginable ways; we have come to love him and appreciate him, but we have not even considered losing him until now. We thought he would be with us a long time, much longer than the life span of our sweet, 12-year old girl, Belle. And he has captured our hearts . . . *every single heart* . . . since this news, I have heard statements like, "He's just the best dog I've ever known," and "This just can't be right. Not Brownie.

I'm not even crazy about dogs, but Brownie is different." I've watched my son hold him and cry, committing to stay with him when the end comes. You see, Brownie might have been something we didn't ask to have, but he is something we have come to cherish.

Which brings me to my relationship with Christ. Christ pursues us, even when we don't know we need Him. He shows up, and we are the ones hanging on the fringes of the yard, needing to be fed and needing warmth, but honestly, not even knowing what to ask for.

(PAUSE here in this writing . . . Brownie is no longer with us as of yesterday. It was a peaceful passing and the right thing to do. He was suffering, and it was time.)

This morning as I write, the Holy Spirit is speaking differently to me, so if you feel like I'm taking a fork in the road in my writing, I am. Just go with it.

Life is filled with unexpected blessings. God brings Brownies into our lives, and they fill spaces in our hearts that we didn't even know needed filling. Sometimes God sends a friend, a surprising relationship, any number of things that touch our hearts and lives in multiple ways. Our response? Accept the blessings, thank God that He sees us and knows exactly what we need, and spend every day appreciating both the gifts and the Giver.

God, the perfect and good Father, wants to give gifts to His children, and so He blesses us. This morning I am looking at the dawn of a beautiful, sunny day. On another day it might be a comforting rainstorm. And on another? Maybe a kindness from a stranger or an answer to a long-lifted prayer. Whatever it is, our job is to accept the beautiful gifts God offers and be intentional about the way we take care of those gifts.

Brownie was an unexpected gift, and just like some people I know, he took a long time warming up to us, but even when he was distant at first, we were faithful to take care of this surprise boy. We fed him and spoke to him from afar. When we first got the privilege of touching him, we did it gently and with loving words spoken over him. As his fearful trembling turned to joyful wagging, we loved him more and more, but we also allowed him time to find his place in our family on Boggy Road. It became his chosen, personal home, and he knew he had found the safest, most loving address ever. Boggy Road = adoptive family.

God has a safe, loving space for us, too. We just need to walk toward Him and let Him bring us into His family. He desires a relationship with every single one of us . . . an adoption into the family of God . . . so He can function as our Father and our mighty Warrior. I love that image. Just like I wanted to protect Brownie, God fights for us and protects us when we stay close to Him, and in a beautifully contrasting thought, He also sings over us just like I often sang and spoke over Brownie.

One more thought: my family is crying this morning at the

loss of Brownie, and we will miss him both individually and collectively in the coming days. But here's what I know for sure: scripture tells us that God cares about our broken hearts, and He holds our tears in His bottle. This morning I am grateful that though I am deeply sad, I am reminded that I am not alone. I am also reminded to be very thankful for the gift of Brownie --- thankful for every day we had him. He made our lives better, and he will go down as one of life's precious surprise blessings.

I encourage you today to examine your life and look around you. See the unexpected blessings and thank God for them. Notice the constant blessings that we often take for granted . . . a warm day, a beautiful sunrise, and a spring season that is upon us. Appreciate the Brownies in your life and do something with your gratitude. This morning, I will speak to a group of women about the power of commitment . . . and I will think of Brownie --- his commitment to us and ours to him. It's a God-lesson I will never forget.

Dreaming of Flying Gifts: Part I

As long as I can remember, I have dreamed of being able to fly, but not in an airplane or helicopter. My body, arms spread wide, soaring freely and gracefully above the bounds of Earth. I remember dreaming about it as a child; I was never way up in the sky, but I hovered a few feet off the ground, gliding with ease. I would wake up, always disappointed that it was not to be.

This morning, as I sipped my first cup of coffee, I watched the birds playing in the sky above the pond behind my house. One in particular caught my eye; I paid closer attention than usual to its flight pattern, comparing it to the very different, almost jagged flight pattern of the birds closer to the house. For a silly, human moment, I was jealous ---- they so beautifully and easily do what I have always desired, but then just as quickly, God gave me a word.

How silly to be jealous of abilities God gave His creatures; He gifted each one of us, animals and humans, with certain characteristics and capabilities that make us distinctly His own creation. How silly and yet, how often we find ourselves jealous of other people who have gifts we do not possess. So, what does God's word say about our gifts and about jealousy?

Well, let's go all the way back to the Old Testament; Moses brought down the Ten Commandments for living --- straight from God. The first four address the vertical relationship between God and His people; the remainder deal with our horizontal relationships with humans. And, number 10? Well, we are not supposed to covet things that belong to others. Coveting goes directly against our trust in God to be all we need, and it creates problems between us and those whose items, abilities, or qualities we are desperate to own. But there's even more reason not to be jealous.

In the New Testament we read in more than one location that the Holy Spirit has gifted each one of us with gifts chosen specifically for us . . . gifts that can be used to glorify God. If the Holy Spirit determined that I should or should not have a particular gift, who am I to question? How dare I be jealous, even of others who can "fly"? Our jealousy and coveting speak to our lack of understanding of the precious gifts with which we have been adorned. Some gifts have been given to all of us, and our job is to develop those gifts within us. An example is the ability to love; other examples are gentleness, kindness, and self-control. We each have all of these and more (found in Galatians 5: 22-23), but we do have to work to develop them in ourselves through study, prayer, and practice. Other gifts that we are given differ from one individual to the next --- gifts like teaching, or prophecy, or healing, or leading. Every one of these is to be honored as a gift from God, given through the Holy Spirit, and we are expected not only to use our gifts for His glory, but to honor the gifts of others, never having a jealous spirit. In other words, if your neighbor can fly, don't be saucy! You are gifted by a perfect God who knows exactly what He called you to do.

So, what is your response? Know yourself as God knows you. Recognize the things He has called you to do because you are more than able. Praise Him for the precious gifts you have received. After all, in the words of David, the Psalmist, "I will praise You because I have been remarkably and wondrously made." (Psalm 119:14a, CSB)

I may not be able to fly, but I am surely flying with Christ ---- not jealous, but grateful that He lets me soar on the wings of eagles, serving Him and glorifying His name is ways I could not even have imagined!

Satan Is A Liar
Know Who You Are In God
Gifts: Part II

Satan is a liar, and he would like nothing more than to destroy our confidence in who we are as God's children. When he steals our confidence in who God created us to be, he takes a hard stab at our destiny of bringing glory to God, our Father.

Case in point.

Recently, I was part of a Bible study group, and for one of the final classes, we were expected to do something creative. The teachers shared things people had done in the past, and I immediately found myself with a catch in my throat and a weight on my chest. "How will I ever come up with something like *that*? How will I measure up in front of my peers?" My thoughts turned my heart to panic, and in the week following our discussion, I felt completely blank. I began to believe that nothing I could do would be "enough."

But God. (One of my favorite phrases). One morning I was praying, telling Him that I didn't have a clue, and time was running out to make a decision and prepare. As clearly as if He spoke audibly, I heard the Holy Spirit say, "Do what you do." Okay, that was thought provoking, so I began to ask myself, "What do I *do*?" Well, I write and sing and speak and teach and grow flowers and love people. That's what I do. And so, it went from there, and within a very short time, I knew exactly what I would do that would utilize the gifts God has given me and would bring Him glory. On presentation day, Satan tried one last ditch effort to shut me down, but it didn't work. I presented that night, and as soon as I got up to share what I had prepared, I knew I was doing exactly what God had called me to do, and my confidence returned. The night did indeed bring glory to God, not only with what I did but with everything that was presented during the evening. God – Victory. Satan – Loss.

And then there are flowers. Someone recently gave me a geranium as a gift, and though I was grateful, I cringed when I saw it: I will kill it! Now, many of you know me as a flower fanatic, and I am, but I know my strengths and weaknesses. I grow daylilies and lots of succulents, plus tons of other varieties, but there are a few flowers that simply do not thrive in my care, no matter what I do: geraniums are one of those. So, this week I was sitting on my porch, looking at that pitiful geranium and cleaning off the dead parts (yes, I'm killing it), and I thought about my Bible study presentation: do what you do. I don't do geraniums, and so this afternoon, I am gifting that plant to my friend Becky whose geraniums look like they could be in a magazine. I'm sure she will save it, and I will visit from time to time. But here's the lesson in these stories: God has purposefully designed each one of us to do specific things in this life. He has equipped us and created us --- we are fearfully and wonderfully made as His children. And in this creation, He has not given us everything. The Bible is clear about this.

Before you think I'm crazy, yes, there are some things we are ALL to do: love God and love others. Period. But when it comes to gifts, we don't all have them all. Before I understood this deeply about God, I knew it in my heart and as a teacher. Children in my classroom learned in different ways and were gifted very differently. Some were strong mathematically, while others excelled in language. Some were strong leaders with amazing organizational skills, while others were cooperative followers who always did their part. Some were athletically talented, while others learned through music. I'm sure you probably see yourself in my descriptions, but why was this so obvious to me as a teacher? Well, God created each one of these children with gifts, and because I paid attention to my students, I could see their strengths clearly.

So, what does scripture say about gifts? Well, it has a lot to say, starting with 1 Corinthians 12: 4-11:

"There are different kinds of gifts, but the same Spirit distributes them. There are different kinds of service, but the same Lord. There are different kinds of working, but in all of them and in everyone it is the same God at work.

Now to each one the manifestation of the Spirit is given for the common good. To one there is given through the Spirit a message of wisdom, to another a message of knowledge by means of the same Spirit, to another faith by the same Spirit, to another gifts of healing by that one Spirit, to another miraculous powers, to another prophecy, to another distinguishing between spirits, to another speaking in different kinds of tongues, and to still another the interpretation of tongues. All these are the work of one and the same Spirit, and he distributes them to each one, just as he determines."

This is just one of the passages in God's Word that addresses this concept of gifts. So, I leave you with two final thoughts. First, do a Google search and study the other scriptures about spiritual gifts; you will be amazed as you see yourself and others in the carefully selected gifts given by a perfect Father. Second, know who you are and use your gifts to glorify God. He gave them to us to be used, not hidden; He always equips His children for the work He has designed and ordained, and when we submit to His plan, we can be completely confident, not in ourselves but in the God who promises that we are fearfully and wonderfully made in His image!

Lessons from Cinderelly

"Cinderelly, Cinderelly,
Night and day it's Cinderelly
Make the fire, fix the breakfast
Wash the dishes, do the mopping
And the sweeping and the dusting
They always keep her hopping
She goes around in circles till she's very, very dizzy
Still they holler 'Keep a-busy, Cinderelly!'"

This song from the movie *Cinderella* has been playing in my head in recent days. I can hear the mice singing, and I'm feeling a little like Cinderelly. Maybe you're like me, and during this time of social isolation, you've been at home way more than usual. I can't remember a time in many years, if ever, that I have been home quite so much, cooking two to three times a day, and cleaning constantly. "Cinderelly, stay busy! There's more to be done!" And I don't even *like* to cook. There . . . I said it, the thing women aren't supposed to say. I *do not* like to cook; I'm quite functional in the kitchen, but it simply isn't my passion nor strength. And yet, every day I face the kitchen tasks --- cooking, cleaning, washing dishes, and starting all over again. On top of kitchen duty, the dust seems to stay ahead of me no matter how much I sweep or use those magic microfiber cloths that are supposed to make dusting a cinch. Last week I finally hit the kitchen wall, so to speak. I was over it.

But then, God spoke, and today I'm still playing the Cinderelly role, but I feel much better about it. What did He show me? Well, even when it comes to housekeeping, God has a Word, and what better place to find God's wisdom than in Ecclesiastes. Ecclesiastes is considered to be a Wisdom Book of the Bible, concerned with helping readers deal with practical issues of life. One of my commentaries says this: "The book of Ecclesiastes faces the issue of how we can find meaning in life in light of the seemingly futile nature of everything." (*Worldview Study Bible*, 2018). Sounds like exactly what I needed, and so God sent a Word.

"Whatever your hands find to do, do with all your strength . . ." (Ecclesiastes 9: 10a), but there's more. In Colossians, we find these verses: "Whatever you do, do it from the heart, as something done for the Lord and not for people, knowing that you will receive the reward of an inheritance from the Lord. You serve the Lord Christ." (Colossians 3: 23-24). Wow . . . cook as for the Lord? Dust as for the Lord? Wash dishes as for the Lord?

Yes. Everything . . . do it as for God. So here goes my head-talk . . . maybe you need to borrow it if you're feeling like Cinderelly, with never-ending work on the horizon,

"Thank You, God, for this house that needs cleaning. I am blessed to live in a dry, warm home in a place I love."

"Thank You, God, that there is plenty of food in my pantry and refrigerator. Help me to be grateful that I have the privilege of cooking."

"Thank You, God, that I have hot water to wash my dishes. You have enabled us to pay the bills and have hot water for showers and dishes. We are blessed."

"Thank You, God, for the privilege of cooking for the grandchildren who live with us. My mother never got to help with my children because she died so young, and I am grateful that I am building relationships with them around the common table."

I could go on, but you get the point. We can whine and complain about the tasks before us, or we can be grateful that we have houses to clean, children to feed, and food to sustain us. The Bible says very clearly that we are not to complain about anything ---- not even chores --- but in everything we are to give thanks. So, when I put this concept with Colossians, I can keep this Jean-paraphrase in my head, and maybe you will want to borrow it:

"God, thank You for blessing me with a house and people who need my care. Forgive me for whining and help me to always face the tasks ahead with a thankful heart."

Will I always get it right? No. There will be nights that the dishes look like a mountain that my body is too tired to climb. But there's always tomorrow, and I know that I'm better after a night of rest. Those dishes can wait until my heart, mind, and body are ready, and then I really will be able, just like Cinderella, to approach my chores with a smile and a song! I pray you will be as well.

Flawed Characters

Summer is drawing to a close, and in true fashion, my husband and I started the season wondering what we would watch on television after our favorite shows aired their final episodes. Yes, we are television watchers. We both work incredibly hard, and at night, I am too tired to do much of anything after dinner except hang out and enjoy mindless fiction with my guy. So, as I said, summers are usually a frustration because our shows are gone, but this summer, we discovered quite an array of Netflix and Amazon Prime series that captured our attention in a big way. The ones that hooked us were mostly historical fiction, often with a little twist, but always with a pattern we began to notice over time: every single show has a male protagonist who is quite attractive and engaging but seriously flawed. I'm talking *really big* character flaws . . . the kind that cause conflict with others and keep viewers on the edge of our seats, often frustrated and talking out loud to them. One night I said to Dan, "Have you noticed that these guys are all seriously flawed?" Well, of course he noticed. There's Jamie Fraser who can be rash and bullheaded. There's Uhtrid of Bebbanburg . . . same problem. Young, handsome, over-confident, and rash. Next, we discovered a young spy during the American Revolution, and he can't seem to decide between his wife and his old girlfriend. Flawed. And finally, there's the ultimate disaster: Ross Poldark. Again, we see a handsome young man who barrels through life, making less than wise decisions that affect his future and his beautiful wife and child. Last night's cliffhanger did not shock me because I have come to expect his foolishness, but I was still a little angry and disappointed. Couldn't he get it right just one time? Of course not, but are these men any different from many of us?

All of these guys have made me think a lot about being flawed. Broken, cracked, flawed. Call it what you will, but we are all imperfect, flawed human beings, walking through life, sometimes allowing our flaws to hurt those we love most and damage our witness in the world. Let's think of a few.

There's pride . . . Uhtrid is the prime example, but we see pride everywhere, doing its worst in the lives of so many. Just recently in Sunday School, we studied the story of Haman, the Agagite, who had everything he could possibly want, but his pride was his downfall. He simply could not tolerate Mordecai's refusal to bow down to him. He plotted to destroy Mordecai and the Jews, but he was one who ended up on the gallows. Pride really does go before the fall. And then there's jealousy.

Ross Poldark lives in constant jealously, not about his wife, but about his former fiancé. He simply cannot stand to see her with anyone else, and in the most recent episode, well . . . you'll have to watch. He made a really stupid decision based on his jealousy, and we see the same in our lives. We are jealous of the Facebook pictures of perfect families and perfect children, and then we make foolish purchases to keep up with others. News flash: people only post their perfect pictures. Their lives are no more perfect than yours.

And then there's jealously over the success of others, or anger over a past hurt or betrayal. In a favorite movie, *The Count of Monte Cristo*, the central character is bent on revenge, and he plans it like a master. But God . . . yes, God, intervened in his heart. The Count finally remembers that God must be his vindicator and forgiveness is required and necessary if he is ever to experience lasting peace. Another flawed character, but this one gives me hope.

When I see others defeating their flaws, I am reminded that with God, we can defeat anything that has become a cracked and broken stronghold in our lives. Scripture tells us that what is impossible in our human strength is completely possible with God. Will we have flaws? Yes, sin is a reality, but we can take steps toward trusting God and giving Him the most challenging parts of ourselves . . . our pride, our fear, our insecurity, our jealousy, our anger . . . the list is endless, but God's grace is endless as well. We can ask Him to circumcise the very character flaw that attempts to define us and destroy us, and through His love, His Word, and His forgiveness, we can become closer and closer to the flawless person God intends us to be.

Good news . . . Ross Poldark received his wife's forgiveness for a deep transgression that could have destroyed their marriage. He woke up to the truth of his love for her, and she finally allowed herself to be vulnerable with him once again. We can do this with God, too. Jesus is waiting --- offering His forgiveness --- a gift of grace --- and we simply must accept. And our story is so much better than fiction because God can be trusted with our lives and our hearts; we can afford to be vulnerable because He is a good, good Father. We never have to wonder if He will take us back because *we* may be flawed, but *He* is not. His mercies are new every single morning, and He is faithful to His children.

I want to leave you with a beautiful prophecy originally found in the Old Testament book of Isaiah and later read by Jesus at the beginning of His ministry (Luke 4: 18-19):

"The Spirit of the Lord is on me because He has anointed me to preach good news to the poor.

He has sent me to proclaim release to the captives and recovery of sight to the blind,

To set free the oppressed, to proclaim the year of the Lord's favor."

Then He says these stunning words: "Today as you listen, this scripture has been fulfilled." (vs. 21)

Can you imagine being there when a prophecy hundreds of years old was quoted by the very Savior for whom they were waiting?

It's almost too much to grasp, but here's what it means for us: Jesus came to release you from the flaws that break and bind you. He came to give you freedom from sin that pours darkness into hearts and minds. He came to open our eyes to the good news of life with Christ at the center . . . a life in which flaws can be defeated and victory against sin is a daily reality.

Flawed? Oh, yes. But with Jesus, the flaws can be forgiven and repaired. We can be new creatures in Christ, and this truth is better than any TV fiction you will ever see.

Stamina and Grit: A Lesson in Principles

I am married to a workhorse named Dan. When he gets his heart and mind invested in a project, there is no stopping him from sun up to sun down. Whether it's baseball card organization or building a new deck, he has stamina for an end goal like few people I have ever known. He is 71-years old, and his stamina was on my mind this morning during prayer time as I sat outside, looking at his latest project.

Stamina. Perseverance. Grit. Principles we need to learn and model for our children.

His stamina has sent my heart and mind into thinking about the events and situations in my life that have caused me to persevere during long, hard stretches. You know the kinds of things I'm talking about . . . prayers that require a long wait for answers, watching and waiting for our children to grow through life's challenges . . . praying and waiting. And that's the key. Praying and waiting. Let's look at this together.

Years ago, I was a hand-wringer. Maybe you've been a hand-wringer, too . . . it's a sign of worry that won't go away. Maybe you struggle to sleep because your mind runs a thousand miles a minute, rethinking your problems and unanswered prayers. Yep, I used to do that, too. Maybe you call every friend you know, seeking opinions and always hoping someone will say what you need to hear. Been there, done that. And maybe, just maybe, in some situations, you have simply given up. Well, there's hope in this storm of needing to grow some stamina and persevere through the marathon called life. And yes, it's a marathon.

First, prayer is both the foundation and the covering of perseverance. I want to give you two acronyms that basically give you same prayer pattern.

PRAY = Praise, Repent, Ask, and Yield

ACTS = Adoration, Confession, Thanksgiving, and Supplication

In a prior devotional called "Patterns of Prayer," I explained the PRAY acronym. So, I ask you to consider using one of the acronyms above if it helps you to focus your time with God and do more than just give Him your list of wants. Prayer is a foundational spiritual practice, and it draws us into the one relationship that can give us strength and perseverance for the marathon.

Secondly, stamina involves getting into His Word. There are so many scriptures about standing strong, letting God fight our battles, and not giving up. A few that come to mind regularly are those about not throwing away my confidence (Hebrews 10:35) and running the race with perseverance as the "cloud of witnesses" surround me (Hebrews 12:1-2). I could write a whole book about scriptures that give me the push to hang on when my flesh is tired, but instead of *my* list, I would encourage you to find the ones *you* need. Complete a Google search or buy a book that is set up with scriptures by topic. I love Joyce Meyer's little purple book, (*The Secret Power of Speaking God's Word*) and I just recently purchased *The Quotable Tozer* (James Snyder, 2018) which is a topical index of A. W. Tozer's Godly wisdom. No matter how you find the words you need, just find them, write them down, and learn them --- even memorize them. You will need them in your memory when you can't get your hands on your Bible and Satan is trying to convince you to give up. Hide those words in your heart!

We have prayer and God's Word, and those are the first places to go. But God gave us something else vital: He gave us friends. When I am struggling with an issue, I have one particular friend I call. Why her? Because I know beyond a shadow of a doubt that two things will happen: 1) She always answers her phone or calls me back. 2) When she promises to pray, she prays. I have other wonderful friends, but these two factors send me to her number on speed dial when my grip is slipping from that proverbial rope and I need a second set of hands. She is my lifeline in the millionaire game of stamina and perseverance, but I also have other friends who are faithful supporters and prayer warriors, so I reach out to them. Maybe we can't get together, and some of them won't have time right away to check the group message, but they are Christian warrior sisters I can ask to stand in the gap with me. I have done it for them over and over, and we trust each other. Sometimes I need just one, and sometimes I need an army, and so do you. God gave us sisters and brothers who can talk to us, pray *with* us, pray *for* us, and hug us; the Bible is a book about relationships, and God, our Father, gave us our relationship with Him first and others second. Make your support calls in that order! Joyce Meyer says, "Go to the throne before the phone."

Finally, after praying and studying, sometimes we just have to practice being gritty. Grittiness is defined as having the qualities of courage and strength, and just like building strong muscles requires exercise, we also have to grow our strength and courage --- *our grit* --- by ***doing*** it. Get up when you don't feel like it. Pray when you are tired. Ask God to give you enough grit for this day alone. Talk out loud to Satan, telling him to get out of your head, and replace those negative thoughts with the words of scripture you have learned. Remind yourself that you serve God, a mighty warrior who saves and the One who can do the impossible! Ask God to send His angels to protect you! Do the things that drive Satan out . . . pray for your enemies, have faith, refuse to quit. Sometimes we just need to rest a moment and get gritty!

In the last two years, I have faced some junk . . . terrible, discouraging junk. Some of the junk was mine alone, some was family junk, and some was junk I was facing right along with the rest of you. A son who almost died, a daughter who moved home with her two children, disappointments at work, a husband with cancer, difficulties in my marriage

. . . a barrage of junk. And, of course, we have all faced hurricanes and pandemics – junk that caused us to hold on until the worst was over. This morning during my prayer time, I felt a clear and powerful revelation; I felt God saying, "You've made it through two very hard years, and where are you now? Still standing and closer to Me than ever before." He's right. This pandemic, as horrible as it has been for the world, has given me time to pray with more diligence and listen quietly to God's voice. When we first started home-schooling four of our granddaughters, I thought, "Wow, this is fun but it could be a long, few weeks." Well, those "few" weeks turned into months, and here we are. But again, I'm still standing, and so are you. God has reminded me today that we need to look back in remembrance at all the things He has done for us in the past. We need to look at today and see how far we have come with His grace and strength. We need to reflect on His goodness and the grit He has placed within us when life has seemed overwhelming. And oh, yeah, we need to do one more thing. Remember the acronyms? Well, in PRAY . . . Y stands for yield. When we yield to God's will, His timing, and His plan for our lives, we will find the grace, strength, and stamina to do whatever He is calling us to do. It's all about surrendering to His plan and His way.

One last revelation. This week I looked out to view the blossoms in my daylily garden, and they were all gone. The deer caught me because I got complacent, and now my field is no longer the beautiful, colorful bounty it was just one week ago. But there's something I noticed, which brought me to this writing: I did what I had to do to keep them from coming back, but I never lost my peace. I haven't cried, and I haven't thrown a pity party. I reflected instead on the reason for my peace, and it's clear: Jesus promised us peace that is not worldly but Godly, and I have it. I have developed the ability to walk in peace by persevering in the worst of moments, learning God's Word, listening to His voice, and surrendering to Him completely. I have grown more than I can explain, and peace is one of the great rewards. Praise God for His magnificent grace and peace!

GRIT (Jean's version!) = Growing Righteousness in Trials

An Open Letter of Prayer

My mother died when I was a young adult. She was a Godly woman, but she was also very private. She kept her Bible by her bed, and she always made church a priority in our lives, but her prayer life was private. Fast forward many years, and I remember asking my Daddy a question: "Daddy, did you and Momma always pray for me?" He looked totally surprised and answered with no hesitation, "Of course. Every day and I still do. Why do you ask?"

Well, I asked because I knew they did, but I needed to hear it said. By the time I became a young woman and began growing in spirituality, my mother was gone, and I never got to ask this most urgent question.

So why am I telling you this? Well, I pray for my children and grandchildren daily, but I often never get around to telling them my prayers for their lives. Recently, a close friend and I were walking, and she shared a new favorite song. She went on to say that she uses the words of that song, pulled straight from scripture, to pray by name for her children. I loved the idea, and I have been following her example since that day. The song is "The Blessing" by Kari Jobe and Elevation Worship, and it has become a beautiful and meaningful part of my prayer practice. But still, I haven't shared with my family about this prayer. So today I share, not just for them but for all parents, grandparents, Godparents, teachers, and praying friends who pour out prayers for children but maybe never tell them the nature of the prayers. I think our children deserve to know.

The Holy Spirit has been nudging me to write this for days, but He spoke loudly and clearly this morning. I opened my Bible to look for a certain scripture, and on the corner of the page, there was an inset: a mini article about Biblical womanhood. And guess what it said: "And how often do you make your children aware of *what* you are praying for them (which encourages them to act on what you are praying)? . . . caring for your children means offering up fervent, visionary prayers on their behalf." (*HCSB: The Study Bible for Women*). Okay, I got the message: write the piece. Don't you love it when He drops things into place exactly when and where we need them? Oh, yes, I do!

Early in the morning as I ready myself for prayer, I ask Alexa to play "The Blessing," and for me, the prayer quickly begins to flow something like this: (Lyrics lifted from the song):

Asher and Courtni, the Lord bless you and keep you . . . make His face shine upon you and be gracious to you.

Timothy, may the Lord turn His face toward you and give you peace.

Laura and Tom, Hannah and Addelyn, may His favor be upon you and a thousand generations . . . your family and your children and their children and their children.

Jamie and Meredith, Chandler, Olivia and Margo, may His presence go before you and behind you and beside you, all around you and within you. He is with you, He is with you.

Whitney, Lily and Harper, in the morning, in the evening, in your coming and your going, in your weeping and rejoicing, He is for you. He is for you.

Jake and Genny, He is for you, He is for you, He is for you, He is for you.

Amen and Amen.

Now to be clear, I pray each part of the song for every child and grandchild, but you don't want to read that long, and I think you get the idea. But there's more: this is surely not just for parents. I have walked the educational road with many young people over my forty years of teaching, and I have loved them deeply. Just yesterday I saw a Facebook post from one of them: he and his wife just had a beautiful new baby boy. This morning I know that I will add them as well as others to my prayers.

Parents and grandparents, aunts and uncles, friends and members of the body of Christ: if you have not told the children you know and love about your prayer relationship with God, the Father, and shared your prayers with them, do it.

Do it now! Do it often! I will never let my children wonder, "Did my Momma pray for me?" Oh, yes, she did. Let it be said that this Momma wore out her knees in prayer for the family God blessed her to have during her earthly journey. I am so grateful that God allowed me to have all of you in my life and to know with complete confidence that He loves you more than I.

Right Spot - Right Time
They Make All the Difference

In December 2019, I bought myself a stationary bicycle. A simple bike --- not one of those fancy ones that talks and tells you what to do. Just a pretty, aqua stationary bike that logs my time, distance, and calories burned. And then, as I have done with other pieces of equipment before, I put it together and looked at it for months. Looked at it, as in, I *didn't* ride it. I put it near windows, thinking I would be motivated by the view. Didn't happen. I beat myself up for wasting yet another chunk of money, even though it wasn't very expensive. I was still wasting what I bought.

Enter quarantine and a new deck space, and everything has changed!

In adding to our existing porch, I was able to un-clutter the original porch, and I decided in a moment that must have come from God that I should move the bike to the porch. I placed it in the shade, facing toward the big pond and in view of my hummingbird feeder, and the bike's new placement has been a complete game changer for me. I ride at least every other day, early in the morning before the heat is unbearable, anywhere from twenty minutes to my highest, forty-six minutes. I use the time to listen to books on Audible, pray, or praise God through music on Alexa. During my latest ride, I observed two hummingbirds, playfully chasing and stopping to eat. My heart was so full! And on top of that, I finished a book that has been important to me: *Be the Bridge* (Latasha Morrison), a book about racial reconciliation.

Learning, burning calories, praising and worshiping God and loving the bounty of nature! What made the difference? Two things: location and time. These same principles, when applied to prayer and Bible study, can make all the difference in your spiritual journey.

I once learned an acronym about Bible study from Priscilla Shirer, and right this minute I can't recall the whole list of words. What I do remember is that she emphasized having a designated spot set aside for studying and prayer. Now, this is not to say you can't study and pray anywhere and anytime; she just suggested that when we make an intentional space, complete with our materials and the solitude for prayer and study, we find ourselves gravitating there, compelled by Christ and our perfect spot to meet Him. In my house it's a rocking chair in a quiet corner under my favorite lamp. I have a small table for my coffee and devotional books and a basket for other materials. I also have a footstool and a cozy blanket, and there are beautiful green plants all around me. My favorite writing utensils are in the desk of the small table, and I can hear Alexa playing praise music while I study and pray. It's a perfect place, and when my family awakes and sees me there, they know *exactly* what I am doing: hanging out with God and His Word.

You see, the place makes the difference. Time matters, too.

For everything in life, we seem to have appointment calendars . . . dentist appointments, hair appointments, meetings to attend . . . exact times we need to be somewhere or do something we deem urgent. Why should this be different in our relationship with God? Doesn't He deserve an appointment time in our schedule, and shouldn't it be the most urgent appointment in every day? Shouldn't it be *first* in the day? Okay, I'm an early riser, so don't hate me. Maybe your appointment with Him is later in the morning, but whenever it is, it should be established and kept. Just like we lose out when we miss a hair appointment, we surely lose out when we don't meet God every single day. What good is perfect hair with an imperfect life?

Now, I'm going to let you in on a secret: I am NOT legalistic. If I miss a bike ride or my Bible study time, or I feel the need to move it to a different time of day, it's okay. God is there all day, every day, waiting on us, and we can chat with Him through our thought-prayers if our more extended time has to be moved or adjusted. You can't be legalistic either. You simply need to be genuine about your love for Him and your desire to spend time with Him, and then? You need to do it! Try to stick to a general time because it helps you develop the spiritual discipline of prayer and study. Do it before the "heat" of your day gets the best of you. But guess what . . . if time gets away and you don't make it to your perfect spot, God's grace is bigger than any choice you make, big or small. His grace is always greater than our sin and our failures, which makes me want to be with Him more and more!

I've been riding my stationary bike for almost four weeks now. I feel better, and my legs are stronger. Some days I think I can't go more than five minutes, but then I ask Alexa to play my favorite Christian praise music or I turn on my Audible study book, and it's amazing how long I can ride. The same thing is true for your prayer and study. Start small; read His Word; talk to Him about everything that matters to you . . . *everything*. And before you know it, your five minutes will be longer than you ever thought possible, and your spiritual legs will be stronger with each ride with God. Place and time: give them to God and watch your life change forever!

Gifts That Match the Receiver

Anyone who has known me for any amount of time knows that I love flowers. I have a deck and porch filled with beautiful plants, and my yard has flowers everywhere. We own a small daylily farm, and I love taking care of the beautiful growing plants and flowers God has created. Recently, two friends gave me plants from their yards. The moonflower, which I was given first by Dian, has bloomed, and the purity of the white blossom took my breath away. Later, I was given some amaryllis. They were extremely tall --- bigger than any I have seen --- and I planted them within view of my back deck. I didn't expect anything from them this year, but I watered anyway, and this morning I received the most beautiful gift: they are blooming and gorgeous! They're the most lovely shade of pink, and I immediately took pictures to send to Heather, the friend who graciously gave them to me. Both Heather and Dian shared these gifts because they know I love flowers, and we flower-lovers understand each other. Joy comes from watching plants bloom and grow. (A little *Sound of Music* "Edelweiss" reference for people my age!)

God knows exactly what gifts we need as well, and He loves to give to us, His children. In fact, scripture says this in

James 1:17: "Every good and every perfect gift comes from the Father of lights." And in Luke, we read another verse about gifts: "If you then, being evil, know how to give good gifts to your children, how much more will your heavenly Father give the Holy Spirit to those who ask Him?"

Perfect gifts for His imperfect, messy children. He gives them daily; we just need to pay attention to what He's doing around us and for us, and then we need to thank Him.

Sometimes the gifts God gives are huge --- an answered prayer or financial relief. Sometimes they are small, but beautiful --- an unexpected blossom on a flower from a friend. At other times, it is the gift of simply feeling His presence and knowing His great love for us. And of course, there is the gift of the Holy Spirit: the one left with us, within us, who guides and directs and instructs us daily. What a gift left when Jesus returned to heaven!

Gifts given from a Father to His children simply because He loves us, and I believe He loves watching us receive all the things He sends our way.

But there's sometimes a problem on our end. We get so busy with life that we miss the gifts He is sending --- gifts meant to bless us and put smiles on our faces. We miss the beauty right outside our window or the flower blooming against the house. We miss the kindness from a stranger, not even realizing that God sent that person to us to bless us. We miss the chance to thank Him for answering the very prayer we asked. Why? We get so wrapped up in ourselves and our lives that we fail to slow down and notice the gifts all around us. He is giving; we need to pay attention and receive.

When that amaryllis bloomed this morning, it wasn't just a gift from Heather. It was a gift straight from God. You see, I've been a little discouraged in the last week or so. I have seen and heard so much hate and negativity, and I've battled with some unanswered prayers. Satan has tried hard to use the problems of the world and home to discourage me, but through a well-timed devotional this morning and those unexpected blossoms, I heard God say, "Jean, you are not alone, my daughter. Notice the gifts sent out of love and be strong in Me."

Yep, that's what I heard, and now, I can feel the discouragement dissipating . . . slipping away quietly as I worship and thank Him for the presents . . . and *THE* Presence. You see, God knows me, His daughter, and He knows exactly what gifts will speak to my heart and lift my spirits. Gifts of words and gifts of nature's beauty. He knows me. And He knows you, too.

Slow down today. Talk to God, pour out your heart, and then pay attention. Those perfectly chosen gifts will come pouring in faster than Amazon can deliver your next package, and I'll be willing to bet that His gift will feed your spirit a whole lot more than the package at your front door. Remember: every good and perfect gift comes from the Father of lights. What beautiful gifts, indeed!

Destiny Is All

I love action and adventure movies and television shows. I especially love ones with strong characters and all the elements of classic stories: love, heartbreak, revenge, redemption . . . you know the ones. One of my favorites of 2020 has been *The Last Kingdom*, a Netflix series that I could watch over and over. Uhtred of Bebbanberg will forever be a favorite male protagonist of mine, and he uses a phrase in every show: *"Destiny is all."*

Destiny is all. I couldn't agree more.

From walking with God for many years, I have learned a lot of spiritual truths, but one of the urgent ones is that God has been preparing me for my current and future assignments --- my destiny --- for years. I learned this in the Bible in many places, and David is a prime example. David was a shepherd; he grew up, learning to be fierce and protective of his animals. When the time came for him to fight Goliath, he knew exactly how to attack, and he was not afraid. He trusted in God completely, and God gave him the seemingly impossible "gigantic" victory. After David was anointed as the next King of Israel, many years passed before he took the throne. During those years, God was preparing, growing, and maturing David so he would be ready to be God's King of Israel in the lineage of Jesus. David's destiny.

God is doing the same thing for you and me.

I began writing in 2009, led by the Holy Spirit to write the thoughts and ideas He whispered to me, but my writing journey began many years ago. God prepared me with phenomenal teachers who pushed me to write well and who taught and demanded proper grammar. During my years of teaching ELA in public school, I taught writing. My supervisor would often tell me that I needed to be writing in a journal regularly in order to be a truly great writing teacher. I didn't disagree, but I also didn't feel that I had time to journal while trying to work full time, raise a house filled with children, and be a good wife and servant at church. When I finally found time and succumbed to the idea of journaling in 2006 (thank you, Joyce Meyer!), it began to change me. My journaling journey is a topic for another day but suffice to say that journaling led to writing which eventually led to publishing my first book in 2014. I never imagined I could write and publish a book, but you see, God had been preparing me for that future assignment for many long years, and when the opportunity came, I was ready. Destiny is all when it is designed by God.

At the time of this writing, it is July of 2020, and I, along with many of you, have been home almost totally since mid-March. During this isolation, I have participated in a Bible study in order to be able to volunteer at a local women's center that ministers to pregnant women, guiding them away from abortion. I have also trained with a local task force concerning how I might volunteer to fight against sex trafficking. But during all of this, I have continued to feel a tug from the Holy Spirit about serving in another area that has burdened my heart for years, and just this morning, I have asked God to show me the destiny He has in store for me and my service.

Destiny is all when designed, chosen, and prepared by God, and I want nothing more than to be walking in my God-given destiny every single day. I'm not suggesting that it can only be one thing. Sometimes God has many plans in store for us, and sometimes those plans change with the seasons of life. For eleven weeks I taught four of my granddaughters when school closed due to the pandemic. Destiny? Yes. I was home and able to allow my daughters to work without worry. God placed me at home when my college classes switched to a virtual platform; He made sure I was available when the time came for me to meet that need.

So, what about you? Are you walking in your destiny that God has ordained? Have you prayed about His will for you? If you feel an uneasiness in your spirit, it could be time to ask God if there are tasks from which He wants you to remove your hands and time to give yourself to a new thing He is preparing you to do. If you are walking in your destiny and know you're in the perfect flow of God, then stay there, but always be open to what He could be calling you to do next. Be an author . . . see a need and meet it . . . teach a class . . .

volunteer your time to ease the suffering of others . . . whatever He is calling and preparing you to do. And remember this as well: God almost always uses your suffering and pain to help others with whom you can empathize. Your suffering is never wasted, so again, ask Him how you can use what you have survived to make a difference in the life of another. He is waiting on our obedience --- destiny, truly, is all.

Progress, Not Perfection

During the summer of social isolating, my husband agreed to build us an outdoor living space --- a place for rocking and reflecting and reveling in family. In addition, I decided it would be a great time to move my stationary bike outdoors. You see, I bought it at Christmas, but buying was all I did. In having space to move it to the porch, I started riding regularly, and just this morning I was struck by a thought, clearly from the Holy Spirit: life is about progress, not perfection. Before these last six weeks, I would attempt to ride the bike, but my legs just felt like lead. Seriously. I would ride for two or three minutes and give up, but now I can ride without exhaustion, some days riding between thirty and fifty minutes! How is this possible? Well, finding the right space and atmosphere made a huge difference, allowing me to make slow progress, even when feeling the effects of summer humidity in South Carolina. I started with about ten minutes a day, and I made progress over time. It took perseverance, but now my legs feel strong and I thanked God just this morning for giving me new strength.

Progress . . . not perfection. Our lives must be measured by the same ruler.

Jesus was perfect, but Scripture clearly tells us that *we are not* . . . will never be . . . perfect, that is. Scripture also tells us that when we stay close to God, Jesus, and the Holy Spirit, through Word and prayer, we can make progress. In theological terms, this is called *sanctification*.

When we accept Christ as Lord of our lives, He justifies us. Justification is the process by which He makes us "right" with God. His blood took away our need to die for our sins, and justification means that the spilled blood of our Savior has made us right with God, allowing His unholy people to kneel before a perfect and holy God. It's immediate and it's final. But, it's not all.

We must spend the rest of our lives being sanctified --- being made holy and more like Christ --- every day, every hour, every minute. So how do we do this? Well, first of all, we recognize the work of the Holy Spirit within us. Jesus promised before His ascension to leave us something better --- one who could be within us at *all* times: the Holy Spirit. He is our guide and the one who helps us discern the truth in God's Word; He lives within us to speak God's Word and plans for us, those beautiful plans to prosper us and give us hope and a future. (Jeremiah 29:11). Imagine seeing a person with a bluetooth speaker in her ear; she can hear what it's playing, but we cannot. It is speaking into her mind, and I like to think this is how the Holy Spirit works . . . our own personal bluetooth speaker! He speaks only what the Father says, and we can hear and trust His voice as He leads, nudges, corrects, and guides. What a wonderful, trusted friend, and there's more!

Another way we participate in our sanctification is by studying the Word. When we study scriptures, we know God more. We learn about His character, which enables us to trust Him completely. We see His actions and strength across time and people, and we learn to allow Him to be in charge of everything. We learn from the stories of David to trust God in the valleys of life. We learn from Moses to trust God, even when we don't believe in our own abilities. We learn from Mary, the mother of Jesus, to submit to God's plan, even when it makes no human sense. Reading and meditating on the Word sanctifies us as we grow spiritually from every story and every piece of instruction. But none of this would be enough without the blanket covering of prayer.

If you read in Ephesians about the armor of God (Ephesians 6: 10-18), you read about all the pieces of protection we have at our disposal. But we can't stop with just the armor, even though it is mighty and powerful. Just after the armor descriptions, we read this: "And pray at all times in the Spirit." It's not an "add-on" or an option. It is the powerful covering for the pieces of the armor of God. It is our relationship builder with God and Jesus. It is the listening guide with the Holy Spirit. It is our time at the feet of the one who can transform us from sinner to servant . . . sanctification. Through prayer we find the peace Jesus promised to leave us --- peace in a troubled world. Through prayer we hear the voice of God, a beautiful whisper or a mighty clap of thunder. Through prayer we submit ourselves to God during the difficulties we face in life, knowing that God will never leave us or forsake us. Through prayer we intervene for others, God's way of making us less self-centered and placing our minds on the needs of those around us. Through prayer we walk into the holy of holies and spend time with the Creator of the universe and the Savior whose blood made all of this possible. Through prayer we pour out our praises, our worship, our tears, and our gratitude, entrusting all to a perfect Father and Savior. And here's a secret: there is no set way to pray. Jesus gave us a model if you are struggling to pray today, and His model is perfect (Matthew 6: 9-13). However, He had a lot more to say about prayer . . . ask in His name, pray with persistence, pray in secret, pray with faith. Notice that it never says "pray with perfection." No, God just wants us to go to Him in prayer. Sometimes all I can say is, "God, I'm having a hard day, and I need You." Other times, I have a lot more to say, and sometimes I just listen. But here's what I know for sure: intimacy with God through prayer is a life-changer . . . a spiritual practice that draws us closer and closer to the women and men He desires us to be: sanctification.

So, don't beat yourself up for not being perfect; that decision was made long ago. In a personal life example, I try very hard to eat carefully and exercise regularly, but I have learned that I *will* make mistakes, and I will still make progress. Remember: it's about progress that occurs when we cooperate with God as He sanctifies our lives, that we might glorify Him and serve Him well. He uses flawed people who simply desire to be all He has designed us to be, and that gives me tremendous peace as I accept myself as His daughter --- not perfect but made right in His sight.

I encourage you to write in a journal. I keep a gratitude list going all year, and many of the items I write show my progress over time . . . sometimes a very *long* time. Writing my gratitude also keeps me focused on what's good in my life and helps me to put my eyes on God's blessings. I don't write every day . . . no perfection here! But I write, and I thank Him, and I keep trusting the process, knowing that progress is good enough for me.

One Degree ---
It Can Make the Difference

There is a motivating video that I've watched many times called "212 Degrees." It's from a website called SimpleTruths, and the basic tenet is this: "At 211 degrees, water is hot. At 212 degrees, it boils. And with boiling water, comes steam. And with steam, you can power a train. Just one extra degree makes all the difference." I watched this when I was part of a school team, looking at every way possible to make a major difference in the educational lives of children of poverty. I have continued to use this video with my students at CCU, wanting them to learn early in their teacher training that teaching children is always about being willing to put forth that extra degree of effort. So, let's think about this in our spiritual disciplines because I believe it is indeed a simple truth worth considering.

Think about your daily routine. Do you spend five or ten minutes reading a quick devotional before you start your day? That's wonderful, but maybe you could you spend five or ten more minutes reading directly from your Bible. One extra degree but an important one.

Maybe you pray a quick prayer in the morning on your way to work. Could you bump it up a degree by turning on praise music while you get dressed, allowing the music to lead you into worship first thing in the day? Maybe you could get up just ten minutes earlier than normal and add a few moments of silence, just listening for God's voice and direction for your day. Just a few more minutes . . . just a small degree of difference.

Or maybe you see prayer requests on Facebook or Instagram, and you think you will remember to pray for each need, but you quickly forget. Turn it up a degree by keeping a quick list in your journal or on your phone so you will remember to pray as you promised. Just that small change can make a difference for you and those whose names you lift to God.

Maybe you listen to your radio on the way to work, but why not change your station to The Message or K-Love or HIS Radio or another Christian station? I found that by making this small change, I was able to go into work with a more positive spirit and a song in my heart. One small degree, but a major difference that powered me through my day.

Sometimes we think in life, work, and our spiritual disciplines, that we need to make dramatic changes, but that's not always the case. I have changed my eating habits in recent months, and I have made some one-degree adjustments that have made a huge difference --- cutting out nighttime eating, smaller portions, and less sugar. Each one of these is just a degree or two, but when added together, they have powered me toward a healthier body and better habits. The same is true with exercise. We don't have to go to the gym for an hour every day to get moving. I made a commitment long ago to park far away from stores and walk more, to always take the stairs, and to increase my number of steps every day. Yes, I ride my stationary bike as much as possible, but sometimes I only ride for ten minutes, and I will take a short walk multiple times during the day.

Small things . . . 1-degree changes that make a positive impact.

Today, I encourage you to take an inventory of where you can heat up your spiritual practices by just one more degree at a time. Remember: that one-degree difference makes water turn to steam and can power a steam engine. One more degree might be the power you need for a fuller, more abundant life in Christ, and with Him, anything is possible!

Not in Our Nature

I have already shared that I have two outdoor cats that I call my "farm" cats. Fuzzy and Cora have been with me almost a year now; they were a gift from a wonderful young woman who had rescued them and nursed them back to health but could not keep them. They are quirky, and I love them. Fuzzy is the hunter of the two, and recently she did something quite interesting that I shared in another piece: she brought a baby bird to us and dropped it in the house. The hunting is not new, but the fact that she brought this bird to us alive was quite a surprise. It's simply not in the nature of a cat to catch a bird and allow it to live. I believe Fuzzy did this because she loves us and enjoys bringing us "gifts" she catches in the yard. Think about that: she did something not in her nature, but she did it out of her love for us. So I want to share some other insights from this odd cat story.

Isn't this just like our lives with Christ? We are able to behave and love in ways that simply are not in our sinful, selfish nature, but out of our deep love for Christ, we can function outside of our natural beings. Let's think about this.

In the New Testament we read about Saul, a murderous killer of Christ followers. He was doing his job, and he did it well.

In fact, just before he left for Damascus in the account found in Acts 9, he was "breathing threats and murder against the disciples of the Lord." But then Saul was blinded on the road to Damascus one day --- blinded by a sudden light and surprised by the voice of the Lord --- and it changed his nature forever. He not only stopped persecuting followers of the Way, but he became one! Not in his nature, for sure, but God changed him. He went on to write a great portion of the New Testament, even writing from imprisonment brought about by his commitment to Christ.

And then there's Zacchaeus (Luke 19:1-10). Remember the "wee little man" from childhood church songs? He was a tax collector, and that immediately placed him in a group of untrustworthy men in his day. Tax collectors were not known for their honesty, and they often took more than was required from the people. But when Zacchaeus met Jesus, he immediately changed his behavior, giving back even more than he had taken from the people. One encounter with Jesus and his old nature was changed because he chose to follow the love and example of a radical man named Jesus.

There's one more because I love to take every opportunity to talk about the woman at the well (John 4:4-26). You know her story, and maybe you've even felt like her before . . . avoiding people because of feeling like an outcast. Avoiding people who might call out your sin. She went to the well in the worst heat of the day when others stayed home, but it was a set up for a change up. Jesus was there, and the beautiful conversation between them sent her running back to town to tell others about this man "who knows everything I have ever done." Her testimony was an immediate change in her nature of avoidance to her new nature of being hungry to tell others of the hope of Jesus.

So, what does this say about us today? Well, if these people could be changed by an encounter with Christ, so can we. We can learn from Old and New Testament stories of God's grace, the life of Christ, and the teachings in the Word about how to put away our old natures and become new people in Christ. Scripture says it this way: "Therefore, if anyone is in Christ, the new creation has come; the old has gone, the new is here!" (2 Corinthians 5:17). Of course, the Bible is a book of relationships, so it instructs us on how to be in a new relationship with God, Jesus, and the Holy Spirit, but it also teaches us to how to be in healthy relationships with other people, NOT in our old nature, but completely possible with God as a new creation.

In Galatians 5:22-23, we read about the fruit of the Spirit: love, joy, peace, patience, kindness, goodness, faithfulness, gentleness, and self-control. These simply are not in our fleshly nature, but when we live in relationship with God, we can develop this fruit in ourselves, allowing God to transform us into people who glorify Him every day. Will it happen overnight? I seriously doubt it, unless God decides to blind you with a sudden light! But we can change over time, working daily to be who God is calling us to be as His children, seeking His strength and leaning into His Word.

How do I know this for sure? Well, He has been changing my nature for years, and He will do the same for you. Not in our nature, but definitely in the nature of our omnipotent God!

Dressing Like Mom

My granddaughter, Olivia, is ten years old, and this year she reached the point that she is almost as tall as her mom and can wear her shoes. She loves being able to share with her mother, and she's not the only one who wants to be like mom. We have three other grands who live on our Boggy Road property, and though they are not quite big enough, they love dressing up like mom. Lily loves to wear her mom's heels, and Harper loves to put on mom's dresses. Margo is only five years old, but she still loves to dress up to "look" like mom, using what they call "fancy" clothes from her cousins' closet. I love seeing them play dress up, and it is heartwarming, of course, that they want to emulate their sweet mothers.

Their play reminds me of an urgent spiritual principle: we need to "put on" Christ every single day, dressing and living just like Him. In Romans 13:14, we read this in The Message: "Dress yourselves in Christ and be up and about!" Another translation puts it this way: "Rather, clothe yourselves with the Lord Jesus Christ, and do not think about how to gratify the desires of the flesh." (NIV). So, what does this mean?

Well, first of all, I believe it means that we must allow our outer selves to reflect Him: our outer appearance and behavior. Are we supposed to dress like He did years ago? No, I don't think so! But we are supposed to dress in a way that reflects our faith . . . as women of God, we are to dress modestly in order not to draw sin into our lives and to, in the words found in Ephesians 4:1, "walk worthy of the calling you have received." (HCSB).

Our behavior in front of others is another outward showing of being "clothed with Christ" (Galatians 3: 27). Are we treating others with genuine kindness and patience? Are we truthful in all our dealings at work and with family? Are we loving others who might be difficult to love? Are we forgiving people as we have been forgiven? Are we walking in humility, not arrogance and pridefulness? All of these can be outward and visible signs of our "putting on Christ" and allowing His light to shine as we journey through life.

There are also inward ways we put on Christ. When we deal with our own sin before God, we are putting on the behavior Jesus commanded. Now, I know He never sinned, but He did go to His Father for everything, even asking if the cup He had to bear could be removed. Jesus taught us by example to go to God.

In addition, we must put on Christ in our hearts and minds. Scripture tells us to study in order that the Word might renew our minds through learning the nature of God and His ways. Jesus knew the Scriptures, teaching them in the synagogue even as a young boy. We are to put on the mind of Christ by knowing the Word and making it the ultimate guide for how we think and live. Through Christ we have the power to choose our thoughts, and what we think determines how we live. When my granddaughters dress like their mom, they are creating a visual image of who they want to be; the clothes create a specific picture. The mind is the same way, and Scripture tells us that what we think about is who we become.

Consider what you "wear" in the coming days. Are you wearing the attitude, patience, and love of Christ everywhere you go? Make an intentional effort to be more patient and move loving at work, in the store, and at church. Just today I was in a grocery store. I know we are supposed to be social distancing, and I was, but the lady in front of me needed to type her card number into the credit card machine, and her eyes were not able to read the digits. I could see the concern on her face and hear it in her voice. I quickly asked if I could do it for her, and her relief was evident. Something so simple but so important as she was standing in line, needing to pay for her groceries.

And consider what else you are wearing? Is it pride? Is it hatred? Ask God to show you what you might be wearing that needs to change. He can give you a whole new wardrobe --- one sewn with love, humility, and grace, and then, the world just might want to shop in the places you've been.

Dress like Jesus, and catch the eye of others everywhere you go.

A 12th Hour Victory

It was the last game of the soccer season, Summer 2020. The season was pushed back from Spring to Summer due to COVID-19, and in July we finally arrived at the end. Harper, my almost 8-year old granddaughter, had loved every minute of playing, having filled the positions of goalie and midfield defense most days. But it was the last game, and Coach Jordan put her in a mid-field position before moving her to striker. It was the last quarter of the last game, and Emory passed Harper the ball. "Kick it, Harper!" Coach Jordan yelled. She did, and it was a perfect kick. It flew over the goalie's head and straight into the net! This might not seem so significant, but you see, Harper had not scored all season. She had weathered the heat and humidity, never missing a game, even when they decided to extend the season. Every game . . . with a smile on her face . . . playing whatever position she was given . . . and then she scores. Last quarter of the last game . . . a 12th hour victory for Harper and her team, sponsored by Grandma's Legacy Lilies. (That's me!)

God gives us the same kind of 12th-hour victories when we are willing to wait with a Harper kind of attitude.

So how can I see this with confidence? Well, look at scripture and you'll see exactly what I mean. In the Old Testament, Joseph was thrown into a well to die, sold into slavery, and sent to prison, but he remained faithful in his heart to the God he loved. And when it seemed like it had been way too long, he was promoted to the most powerful position possible, and it placed in the exact spot necessary, giving him the power and position to save Egypt and eventually his own family from famine. The 12th-hour victory came after Joseph was willing to wait, suffer, and still trust God. I love that story.

And then, there's the woman with bleeding. You'll find her story in the New Testament Gospels. She had been bleeding for 12 years . . . yes, *12 long years*. She had spent a fortune on doctors who could not help her, and she must have wanted to give up. This lady had been suffering for an incredibly long time, but she heard that Jesus was in town. His reputation preceded Him, and she knew that He was her only hope . . . her *last* hope. She got close enough to touch the hem of His garment, and her faith in Jesus was enough: after years of bleeding, she was immediately healed. Jesus questioned who touched Him . . . He felt the power go from Himself to her . . . and then He spoke to her. "Your faith has made you well." Wow, what a 12th-hour healing, to be sure. Both of these stories have a foundation of faith.

And then there are my own stories of 12th-hour victories . . . my son waited months and months for news that could change his life forever. We prayed and prayed; we waited and waited; we got even better news than we expected, and it truly was a 12th-hour victory after nearly two years of waiting. And then there was the Teacher of the Year. I was in the Top 5 for TOY when I was a teacher at Conway Middle School, but it was not my time to win; I had a lot of growing to do. Years later, when I had transferred to Loris Middle School, I found myself in the Top 5 one more time, but this time, God had a different plan. I won, and my victory became "our" victory for the children of LMS. They greeted me in the schoolyard the day after I was announced as TOY, saying "We won!" They knew it was a *team win* . . . a 12th-hour victory for a school that needed to know just how valuable it was to its community and children who needed to know they were part of a winning team. God knew exactly when and where this victory needed to happen to have the most important impact --- the impact He desired.

I could tell you more stories of victories that were long in coming, but here's the lesson: during every time of waiting, my job --- Joseph's job and the woman's job --- was to be faithful, trust God, and wait on His timing, which is always perfect. Sometimes He is working on us, maturing us and drawing us close to Him. Sometimes He is changing us or our circumstances so when the victory comes, we are ready to be in the position and more prepared to be grateful. Joseph had to grow up; the woman with bleeding had to be desperate for healing; my son had to be able to see the hand of God; and I had to be more mature and in the right seat in order to represent God in the way He had in mind. I was able to stand before that crowd at the TOY banquet and say with humility and assurance, "I am here for such a time as this."

God has 12th-hour victories in store for every single one of us. So be faithful, be patient, and be willing to submit to His leading, His plan, and His timing. Wait with a Harper attitude as He prepares to score the goal of a lifetime for you and yours.

From Fear to Freedom

We live on a large property in the country, and have created a family compound. Besides having family close at hand, one of the most beautiful elements of Boggy Road is our five ponds. I love to watch the sun gleaming on the surface of the water or the wind moving across the surface until it almost looks like waves. We have some sort of boat on every pond, and I enjoy paddling form one end of the pond to the other, but there's one problem: I can't get my granddaughter, Lily, to get in the boat. She tried the paddle boat one time . . . it was her *last* time! She is an excellent swimmer, so drowning isn't her fear. I think the idea of falling into that dark water scares her to death. The water is filled with fish and turtles and a few otters, but even worse are the grasses that tickle your feet. They are tall, and in certain spots, it can feel like the boat is actually sitting on the grass. Anyway, Lily will *NOT* get in any of the boats, and it's really sad. She could row across the ponds and enjoy the freedom of being away from the shore, slipping silently across the surface of the water. But no, her fear is greater than her desire for freedom.

Aren't we like that sometimes? Do you have fears in your life that keep you from living in the freedom God has called you to enjoy?

Let's swim in this for a moment. (Sorry for the pun.)

Lily lives in fear of the unknown . . . fear of what she cannot see that might be lurking under the water . . . and we can be the very same way. We are afraid to make a decision because we don't know how it might turn out. We are terrified to leave a dead-end job for a new opportunity because we can't see every step of the future. Women stay in abusive relationships because of the fear of the unknown --- a new life without a spouse --- is more terrifying than the known abuse. It's sad, but many people are frozen with fear of the future they cannot see. God has an answer for this particular fear. He tells us to trust Him and Him alone. We read that He is our Father and He loves us more than our earthly parents love us. Scripture tells us that He has good gifts in store for us --- NOT scary endings. But it comes down to spending time with Him, knowing Him as a good, good Father, and trusting that He will always protect us when we step into His boat in faith.

Lily also lives in fear of the darkness of the water. She has absolutely no fear of a swimming pool because she can see clearly to the bottom, but in the pond, the darkness can appear to be frightening even though there is nothing in the dark that can hurt her. Many children grow up feeling this way, asking their parents to leave a light on or leave the door open to the lighted hallway. Why? The dark scares us. And yet, with God, dark can be comforting. I love sitting on my porch, looking at the night sky. When I see the stars and all that God has made, I am awed by His handiwork, and it shines more brightly against the dark. We can do that, too. Instead of running and hiding from the dark, we can face it with God, knowing that He is with us and for us. Sometimes we need to realize that the dark is nothing more than an absence of light. But you see, we serve a Savior who *IS* light --- the light of the world. He can light up our souls so we can move into the darkness in complete confidence. The sky is not more dangerous when the stars are not shining brightly; it's simply darker. We know the stars are still in place and the darkness will eventually go away. We simply have to trust God in the waiting and stop being afraid of what we cannot see.

One day, I know that Lily is going to get in that boat with someone she trusts. It will probably be her mom or dad because she trusts them completely. And I will be on the shore, celebrating for her and watching her row her way to freedom. There's one more spiritual truth: when we trust God, having faith even the size of a mustard seed, we can eventually overcome our fears, get in the boat, and maybe even walk on water a little. God holds out His hand, and the knowledge that He will never let go can create a new bravery in each one of us. Knowing that, should we fall over the edge, He is capable of lifting us up and placing our feet upon a solid rock is some pretty amazing assurance. And if we cry, we have a Father who holds our tears and a Savior who understands heartbreak. This is a foundational truth of our faith; knowing God's goodness and His love for us is a rock on which to build our lives.

So, I encourage you today to get into that boat and row wherever God is taking you. Trust Him to complete the good work He started in you and to take you places that are only for your good. Let Him be in the front of the boat as you row with Him from fear to freedom. I know Lily is going to do this, and I pray you will, too!

Submitting to a New Task

I have never seen myself as a housewife. I don't remember ever waking up and saying to myself, "I want to be a housewife. I want to cook, and clean, and make everything perfect for my family." Be a mom? Oh, yes. I desperately wanted to be a mom, and that prayer was answered. Be a wife? Yes, again. Be a teacher? Yes, yes, yes! But I always saw housekeeping as a necessary entity to being a wife and mother, not something I aspired to do. I did what I had to do but without much joy.

Fast forward to spring and summer, 2020. What a weird and crazy life-changing time! We've all adjusted our patterns of living due to this "thing" called COVID-19, and during this time, I have become the thing I never desired: a housewife. Just last week the thought struck me that I am living in a new routine, and . . . here it comes . . . I like it. Whoa. I never thought I would say those words, and even a month ago, I couldn't say them. But now I can. I now have time to think and plan meals that are better choices for my family and me; I am home to make the bed after Dan gets out (hours after I get up!), and my bedroom has become a place I actually enjoy as a quiet haven of peace. My pantry and grandchildren's play closet are reorganized, the garage has been rearranged, and my flowers on the deck and porch are getting tons of attention. I could tell you many things I do with my mornings now that are different than before, but the point is that I complete these simple tasks and find joy in their completion. What a change!

Submission. That's my new word: submission. I have made a conscious choice to submit to a new pattern of living, and God has blessed my attitude in ways I didn't believe possible.

So, where do we see examples in scripture of people submitting to tasks in humility and joy? Well, the first one that comes to mind is David. I heard a pastor say recently that David was "faithful in the field" while waiting to be King. Remember: he was anointed as King when he was only a young shepherd boy --- the youngest in the family and even dismissed as not an option when the prophet Samuel arrived to anoint God's choice as King --- and he had to submit to continuing as a shepherd for years before stepping into his destiny as King David. God used those years as preparation for his eventual destination: being the King of Israel and being in the line of King Jesus. He submitted to daily practice in protecting the sheep, and his submission to this isolated task prepared him to kill Goliath . . . he took down lions and later took down a physical giant of an enemy. He submitted to his assigned task, and it prepared him for the future God ordained for him long before he even knew he would be King.

In my own life, not only am I in the housewife role, but I am also teaching my grandchildren on the days they are not in school. God has been preparing me for this gift of time with them for years. After all, I have been a teacher my whole adult life, so helping them is easy and joyful for me. I am being faithful in my field on Boggy Road, using my abilities to help ones that matter to me most. I haven't killed lions, but I have survived and thrived in public education; teaching four little girls is a breeze compared to that, but only because I am submitting to God's plan with joy and using what He has prepared me to do for so long.

So, what is God asking of you during this season? Do you find yourself unable to do the tasks you would typically do? How are you responding to having parts of your life and plans "cut off" for a season? In scripture we are told not to complain about anything, and this is a chance to put that into practice! And what about something God might be asking you to do in this season? Do you need to pray about joyfully submitting to staying home, or housekeeping, or teaching grandchildren, or finding new ways to minister to others? Whatever God has tasked you with accomplishing, do it; submit joyfully and get it done. When God gives us new expectations in a new season of life, and we respond with grace, grit, and joy, we truly can become the light of Christ in a dark season. Submit today and shine for Him!

Perseverance and GRIT:
Growing Righteousness In Trials

As I think back over this unusual and trying year (2020), I have found myself thinking back further in my life story. How many times in life have I been challenged to persevere in the worst of circumstances? How many times have I watched people I love during an extended time of waiting and suffering? 2020 has been especially hard, but the concept of facing extremely difficult times in life is not new to any of us.

As I write this final piece, I am thinking of a wonderful young woman I taught who just lost her battle with cancer. It was long and painful, and through it all, she entrusted herself and her future to her God. Her legacy will definitely be how she lived, but also how she faced the great trial of impending death at a young age.

And then I think of my daughter and other young women who find themselves as single mothers, a role I have played myself. For my daughter, it has been two years of learning to do things differently and juggle a life of working and mothering and learning to take better care of herself. Two long years of growing to overcome challenges, and it's not over yet.

I think of self-esteem battles that require years to overcome, marital disappointments, and financial strain brought on by poor decisions or economic failures beyond our control.

I think of my own life. So many times, I have faced deep heartaches that didn't heal or go away as quickly as I would have liked. The loss of my mother, the failure of my first marriage, disappointments in friendships, prayers that didn't receive the answer I expected, long years of praying for specific desires for my children and friends . . . all of these have one thing in common: they have required Godly perseverance --- staying power that I don't have on my own but am allowed to gain through my relationship with Christ.

I read a book last year about the idea of grit, so what is it and what does it have to do with perseverance? Well, the dictionary says that grit is the ability to persist in something you feel passionate about and persevere when you face obstacles. It's passion and perseverance for long-term and meaningful goals. This sounds about right to me, and I love the concept of being a woman with grit. So, let's explore this together.

The more I pondered grit, the more I felt this acronym become clear: GRIT = Growing Righteousness In Trials. We have no righteousness on our own, but God's righteousness has been imputed to us, meaning that we can treat it as our own. This is the concept of justification when we accept Jesus as Savior; then, we spend our lives being sanctified, or growing more and more like Him . . . more and more holy. I believe that when we cling to God, His power, His strength, and His wisdom in the trials of life, our righteousness deepens and grows in ways that can only happen in the valleys and the waiting rooms of life. Valleys and waiting rooms that can be rocky and lengthy.

But God is faithful.

I love Psalm 23, for it says this: "Yea, though I walk through the valley of the shadow of death, I will fear no evil for Thou art with me." (I memorized it in the Kings James years ago!). Did you notice the phrases? We walk through the valley, and we are not alone. We don't have to collapse under the obstacles of our lives because God says we can walk through with Him. Sometimes I suspect that He has to carry us, and I trust Him to do just that. Sometimes we are praying to get out of the valley, but He lets us stay there much longer than we think He should. Sometimes we pray for answers, and they are a long time in coming. So, what is it we learn when it takes perseverance and grit to keep moving?

First, I have learned to trust God, even when it takes what seems like forever or I don't like the pain in which I find myself. He is Father, and He always has good in store for us. We simply have to trust Him.

Second, I have learned that God is often doing things behind the scenes that I can't see, and shifting the sands around me often takes time. We must trust His timing and trust what we cannot see with our own eyes, knowing that our sovereign God sees what we cannot and is working things for our good.

Third, I have learned that I must be obedient during trials. Obedience definitely looks like staying faithful to my prayer relationship with Christ and my study time in His Word. It might also look like doing the last thing God asked of me, knowing that when He is ready, He will give me a new task to complete. Obedience also looks like forgiveness and kindness and praying for our enemies and love for all and peace in the middle of the muck of life, as I await His revelations for me. We must be obedient to Him, even when we don't feel like it.

Fourth, I have learned that I am in one of three places in life: I'm in one of life's trials, I've just come out of a difficult trial, or I'm headed into one. Life will never be trial-free, and if we expect that kind of journey, we are fooling ourselves and not heeding Jesus' words. He said that we would have trials and tribulations, but He also said that we could celebrate because He overcame the world, and so will we.

What is our response? If you are in the middle of what looks like a never-ending challenge, hold on with grit. Cling to God. Give Him your heart, your faith, your love, and your obedience. Know that it will indeed end in His timing. Ask Him to help you grow during the challenge because lessons learned in the valley are lessons worth keeping. And never forget to be thankful --- not for the trial, but in the midst of it.

If you are in a peaceful time without conflict right now, thank Him! Thank Him for your past difficulties and lessons you learned. Thank Him for every tranquil moment. Thank

Him for everything! Take time to write in a journal about your spiritual insights and growth in your relationship with Christ. When you find yourself in another trial, you will be blessed to look back and see the hand of God in everything as you read the pages of your journey. Sometimes we have to look back, remembering His goodness and the lessons we've learned, in order to move forward.

The pandemic of 2020 has been an unusually challenging time for all of us. But here's what I know for sure: I have learned to slow down, and I pray you have, too. I have done things I never believed I could or even wanted to do, but I have done them with joy, and I bet you have as well. I have found peace in my home and my family, and I have found purpose in the extra time on Boggy Road. It has surely been a trial for all of us, and it's not over, but through this trial as any other, we can have grit as we face every obstacle with passion and perseverance, made possible by an omnipotent and holy God.

G.R.I.T.

Growing Righteousness

In Trials

Works Cited

"212 Degrees." https://www.simpletruths.com/most-inspirational-videos.html.

Carnes, Cody, Elevation Worship, and Kari Jobe. "The Blessing." 2020.

Chan, Frances. Crazy Love: Overwhelmed by a Relentless God. David Cook Publishing. Colorado Springs: 2013.

DiCamillo, Kate. Because of Winn Dixie. Candlewick Press. Somerville: 2010.

"Do It Again." Elevation Worship. 2017.

Finklea, Josh. Sermon quotes. The Rock Church. Conway, SC: 2020.

Goewey, Don Joseph. "85 Percent of What We Worry About Never Happens" https://www.huffpost.com/entry/85-of-what-we-worry-about_b_8028368#:~:text=Lo%20and%20behold%2C%20it%20turns,them%20a%20lesson%20worth%20learning. 2015.

Meyer, Joyce. The Secret Power of Speaking God's Word. Warner Faith. New York: 2012.

Snyder, James. L., editor. The Quotable Tozer: A Topical Compilation of the Wisdom and Insight of A.W. Tozer. Bethany House Publishers. Bloomington: 2018.

Spangler, Ann. Quote on Faith Gateway devotional.

Terkeurst, Lysa. Finding I Am: How Jesus Fully Satisfies the Cry of Your Heart. Lifeway Press: 2017.

Terkeurst, Lysa. Twitter quote. 2017 and 2018.

The Worldview Study Bible. (Christian Standard Bible). Holman Bible Publishers. Nashville: 2018.

Viorst, Judith. The Tenth Good Thing About Barney. Aladdin Paperbacks, an imprint of Simon and Schuster. New York: 1971.

Walsh, Sheila. Praying Women. Baker Books. Grand Rapids: 2020.

www.ingramcontent.com/pod-product-compliance
Lightning Source LLC
Chambersburg PA
CBHW021426070526
44577CB00001B/78